GIORGIO GIULIO
CLOVIO

ALPINE
FINE ARTS
COLLECTION, LTD.

Self-portrait, Florence, Uffizi

GIORGIO

MINIATURIST OF THE RENAISSANCE

CLOVIO

Maria Giononi-Visani

Grgo Gamulin

Publishers of Fine Art Books
527 Madison Avenue, New York, New York 10022

Published in 1980 by:
The Alpine Fine Arts Collection, Ltd.
527 Madison Avenue
New York, New York 10022
All rights reserved. No part of this publication may be reproduced or
transmitted in any form or by any means, electronic or mechanical,
including photocopy recording or any information storage or retrieval
system, without written permission from the publisher.
ISBN: 0-933516-17-7
This edition is published in cooperation with
SPEKTAR, Zagreb, Yugoslavia.
Drago Zdunić, Director
This book was produced in Yugoslavia

Battle Between Skeletons and Knights,
detail fo. 119 v, Stuart de Rothesay Book of Hours, London, British
Museum

INTRODUCTION

Grgo Gamulin

Giorgio Giulio Clovio, known as Giulio, was praised during his lifetime as *il più raro e il più eccellente miniatore.* This "rarest and most exellent miniaturist" was then condemned to be forgotten; his work lives on in an artistic limbo, unacknowledged by the world of painting and museums. Clovio's fate was shared by many other artists of the mannerist period in which he worked. Even today, after modern research has revealed the wonderful diversity and originality of that late Renaissance style, and spiritual state, Giulio Clovio still has not found his place.

His work is rarely shown in galleries, and his name finds no mention in compendiums or in theoretical discussions of mannerist painting. ·Yet El Greco himself, the spiritual climax of that same style, in 1570 included Clovio among his four teachers, painting his portrait in the *Expulsion from the Temple* along with those of Michelangelo, Titian, and Raphael. El Greco placed Clovio beside the greatest masters of the *cinquecento,* passing over such better-known painters as Tintoretto and Jacopo Bassano.

Perhaps it seemed to the young Cretan that Clovio, the sole survivor of the four, was the only painter left who still practiced their true art.

El Greco saw in the *Officium Virginis Farnese,* Clovio's masterwork, the concentrated glory of the classical heritage. He was Titian's pupil, and perhaps Clovio's, but he was not an artist who could live in the past and, in Rome, there was no escape from it. At that moment only Venice could provide the artistic freedom essential to his spirit.

Giulio Clovio, on the other hand, was firmly bound to the artistic tradition of the Renaissance. He passed almost the whole of his life thus restricted, living at the courts of his patrons. El Greco, in returning to Venice, returned not only to his "painting homeland", but also to a higher phase of mannerism than that being practiced in Rome. In Venice everything tangentially classical, and especially everything tangentially classicist, had already been assimilated. Only in an atmosphere where "tonal

conformism" had already been surpassed, shattered not so much by the formal crisis of the years around 1540 as by Tintoretto's fantasy of light, could the young Cretan achieve the pinnacle of mannerism in painting.[1]

El Greco, the Cretan, and Giulio Clovio, the Croat, each exemplify one of the directions of Italian mannerism, which was characterized by a basic duality: classicism and anticlassicism, acceptance or rejection of the past. This polarization grew out of deep social motivations and influenced the varying degrees of stylistic and creative freedom in the art of the *cinquecento*. Modern theory has surprisingly achieved an affirmation and recognition of the concept of mannerism, in spite of somewhat sketchy definition. This recognition, unlike that of Gothic or Baroque, has erased mannerism's negative connotations. Clovio is not included in this theory; perhaps his position is too problematic. Several centuries after his death, he lives on only in the treasuries of patrons and collectors.

For this we can blame not only the exclusivity of the miniature as an art form, but also the insufficiently precise understanding of mannerism and of certain basic distinctions within the *cinquecento*. There was a separation between classical art (and its sometimes original and spontaneous, but often "programmatic" imitation, classicism) and the new creative variants of mannerism, in which the eternal artistic problems were posed afresh. If we remind ourselves of how long Tintoretto and El Greco remained unrecognized as mannerists, we need not be surprised that Giulio Clovio was actually forgotten (even by Herman Voss in his, at that time all-encompassing book[2]).

This was before the "resurrection" of mannerism. Today the movement has been divided into several strands and cultural motivations, and each of these again into many individual expressions, forming a variegated map of the late Renaissance. Clovio should find his place here, surely not as a classical artist, but neither as a rebel or some kind of anticlassical heterodox. When we look at the glowing pages of *Officium Virginis Farnese,* or the *Commentary to St.Paul's Epistles* or the *Towneley Lectionary* we find ourselves in the focus of a lens which includes and reflects much of the late Renaissance. It would probably be even more exact to say: a certain part of central-italian mannerism. But is Clovio's work only *a reflection,* or is it that truly *creative reflection,* which any genuinely creative expression of mannerism must be? This is a question not yet answered. Criticism has, in fact, raised the question ever since Kukuljević-Sakcinski and Bradley began their reappraisal of this "last miniaturist". As a phenomenon (and as a problem) it is doubly interesting: the art of the miniature ended its great yourney in the "classical" mannerism (which in this case is not even a *contradictio in adjecto*) of an artist whom El Greco himself placed at the top of the Parnassus of painting of his own time. Modern criticism has also found itself faced with a dual problem: that of the practical difficulties of studying miniatures, which are hard to come by, and of the necessity, before any evaluation of the lifework of Giulio Clovio is possible, of determining more precisely just what mannerism is and what its modifications are. We consider this monograph about the "last miniaturist", along with the study by Maria Cionini-Visani included in it, an important step in overcoming these difficulties.

Perhaps the study of this forgotten artist will even help us to understand this mannerism, whose birth in theory and criticism we have witnessed in recent decades. At least it may begin to clarify the significance of the span of activity between the highlights of the Renaissance, with their conventional echoes, and the turn to a fresh, vigorous mode of expression. Clovio, as well as many others, faced the choice of surviving as an imitator or destroying the past. In the theory of mannerism such moments of decision were observed to a certain extent in the pioneer work of Pevsner, Weissbach and Friedländer, and we also find them in Arnold Hauser's monumental book.[3] Some new views about the wide circle of imitators (which are, perhaps, of special importance for studying moments of imitation in Clovio himself) can be found in Eugenio Battisti.[4]

But why has Giulio Clovio all the same been forgotten in the theoretic context to date, and in the study of that great century? This is a question that future research must answer. Where does his value, or, to be more precise, his stylistic and cultural-historical importance, lie in that extraordinary century, in which great values were destroyed? There were as yet no new values, at least none that could impose themselves forcefully on society and the foci of social consciousness. But in the high temperature of the new religiousness of the Reformation and Counter Reformation, some old values were being renewed. An era of open crisis began after *sacco di Roma* and the fall of the bourgeois Florence (1530). This was a crisis of the Renaissance and of the Renaissance conception of the world, a moment when human impotence began to be felt again even more strongly, destroying the feeling of harmony between nature and human possibilities. The crisis was not only ideological and intellectual, but also psychological: the crisis of a "bad conscience"[5]. In such moments of confusion and imbalance every phenomenon acquires a fuller significance and more acute meaning. What was then, the significance of our artist in that time of doubt and new "relativism", in which even nature could no longer be followed according to the old humanistic and Renaissance rule of "mimesis" (which was, luckily, not mimesis), and in which skepticism permeated human creativity, providing the dynamic impulse of movement and research?[6]

1.

Today we consider that Clovio lived among ruins, but he himself was certain that he was erecting his building on eternal foundations. He was aware neither of ruins nor of that catastrophe with which we, from the time of Dvořak onwards, explain the shifts visible from our "all-encompassing distance".

We are even ready to forget that the four following centuries did not see any signs of ruin either. And Clovio really did start from established and official standards (those given by the most highly acknowledged of Raphael's pupil). *The Last Judgement* (the terrible judgement of art) did not exist as yet in the Sistine Chapel, Clovio knew nothing of the events which started in Florence in the antehall of the Annunziata, to end with Pontormo's despair in the choir of San Lorenzo; or he became aware of them when it was already too late. Obviously he did not feel the world to be a "labyrinth".

All the same, his life had not been easy. Historical misfortune had pursued him from the very beginning: in 1526 he fled to Italy from the Battle of Mohač; the following year he fled again from the devastation of Rome.

He was pursued by infection and disease. He sought refuge in monasteries, and found a home (for himself and his art) with the greatest patrons of the time. At the end of his life, when he came into contact with El Greco's style, that painter of a pre-mannerist style, he understandably saw in him only a "praiseworthy pupil of Titian". Clovio believed that his own art observed the rules of the greatests, that he was continuing classical art of formal ideal and harmony. Today, however, we are forced to compare his work not only with the classics of the Renaissance, but also with the great new discoveries of mannerism. Indeed, his very masters, those on whom he modelled himself, in today's interpretations reveal new dimensions. Thus (also from Dvořak's time) we recognize Michelangelo as the first great artist who was dissatisfied and out of step with the optimistic world outlook of the Renaissance: "His profound enquiring spirit made it (the classically joyful Renaissance acceptance of the world) unacceptable for him and forced him to consider once again — following the deepest currents of the age — the fundamental questions of being: why a man lives and what the relationship is between the transitory, earthly and the eternal, spiritual, values of mankind."[7] This great artist was the stylistic and morphological starting point for Clovio as a mannerist. Does it mean that we must compare them? Is it possible upon such gigantic foundations to build one's own world of forms, which to a great extent means one's art, and still develop oneself as separate and different? This is, of course, not just the problem of Clovio, it is the problem of the whole mannerist movement. Distinctions must be made between mannerism and the mannered, between classicism and anticlassicism, and the assimilation of a copiousness of forms (a formal system, that is) in a new creative spirit.[8]

"The problem of how to apply the principles of others" — isn't it the abyss that opened up before almost all the artists of the *cinqueunto* and upon whose brink they almost all balanced? It is Clovio's problem, too, and it is compounded by the mentioned necessity of comparison with many other artists, rebellious and bizarre, the number of whom increased in this extraordinary century — *nel coro molteplice* — as someone had already said.[9] And so involuntarily we are led into comparisons not only with Clovio's models but also with those who came after him, especially the pinnacle of mannerism — El Greco, who was once Clovio's protégé. Here, as in the case of Michelangelo, we are confronted with something superhuman which renders any artistic comparison almost impossible: "El Greco was a pure idealist" wrote Dvořak about the onetime protégé of Clovio in his "mannerist initiation", comparing him to Cervantes and Don Quixote. "His art marked the height of a general European art movement, the goal of which was to replace the materialism of the Renaissance by a spiritual goal for human aspirations."[10] From these first "dedications" the range of the phenomenon spread to the infinite and the ideas themselves took on another denomination. With what uncertainty, for instance, do we approach the very relative idea of "Renaissance materialism"? And with what spiritual charge today, after so much research and so many interpretations, is this critical century filled?

From Rosso's *Deposition* of 1521 until the time that Caravaggio went to Rome and after that time, phenomena of the most varied meaning mingled and developed through him, and a whole labile construct, formed from several systems (schools, directions, and completely opposing ideas and relationships) and from an almost endless series of painters, filled up the rest of the century.

As the walls of tradition crumbled and collapsed around him, Clovio remained in his small workshop in a monastery or in the Farnese Palace keeping firmly to his paragons. He was not aware of the contemporary debates of the classicists and anticlassicists, for example those of Pietro Bembo and Gian Francesco Pico della Mirandola of 1512.[11] He did not even suspect the importance of the "dialogues on art" (P. Pino 1948, L. Dolce 1957) that, at about the middle of the century, theoretically resolved the great Venetian polarization of the *cinquecento*. At least no echo of these can be felt in his miniatures. He lived and created in the spirit of a secure system of stylistic concepts, even of archetypes. We have no reason to think that he was disquieted by eternal problems of mimesis and reality: can that system comprehend reality, and is it in fact necessary to represent and comprehend reality, or is it (for art) enough to comprehend this system of forms and instruments? If not, how can reality be interpreted "deductively" through a new artistic unreality. The artists of the mannerist movement asked these questions, even if not consciously. These questions signalled the moment of realization of the dramatic insufficiency of the accepted system. The classical Renaissance archetypes had been turned into systems of stereotypes.[12]

Miniature painting, which was at that time considered the "translation of painting", a reduction and, at the same time, a compendium of great creation (great form in small format), now seems to us like a new field of the absurd, as if the inductive Renaissance method of starting from the object was not valid after 1630. Clovio still relied on archetypes and prototypes, and with his unerring instinct for unity of expression, he chose only adequate systems, and those he felt to be interrelated. He included them in all his tasks and conceptions, translating and linking various currents that at first glance seem contradictory: for example, in the very same folio of the most sacred book of Christianity, destined to explain the mystery of the Eucharist at the altar, we find mystical scenes in frames full of pagan beauty and Parmigianino-like eroticism. What can this represent but the general tension of mannerism transferred to the narrow field of miniature art? By means of this tension Clovio maintained a balance which kept him from being swallowed up by the absurdity of his situation. He ignored the clash between classicism and anticlassicism, achieving instead a serenity and spiritual homogeneity which buttressed and strengthened his art.

But this has only been to indicate the problem of Giulio Clovio. To understand Clovio's significance in the frame of mannerism (just such a *mannerism*) we must find a working definition of the term, as well as a method of analysis that will enable us to reevaluate his work.

To do this we may have to return to the basic definitions of mannerism, perhaps even to an analysis that will help us in the evaluation, or the re-evaluation, of Clovio. We do not need here to carry out any kind of recapitulation of mannerism either in its historical actuality or in its theoretical reflection. Generalizations such as those that consider mannerism as the "common denominator of all currents contrary to classicism" can be of little help to us. Curtius' definition of mannerism as the "common denominator of all currents contrary to classicism"[13], is no longer valid even as a generalization. As Eugenio Battisti wrote, "The most diverse phenomena are classified under figurative mannerism." But not everyone was conscious of a crisis, nor did crisis have the same meaning for everyone. It is very probable, for instance, that Giulio Clovio was not conscious of any crisis, least of all any crisis of classical art.[14] But for us his position remains poised between classicism and the Counter Renaissance classicism being derived and thus different from true classical art.[15] It is furthermore a problem of authority and revolt, order and disorder, but these notions are unstable and conditional. For how could Clovio, who throughout his long life had believed in authority and followed an order of things and harmonies, cease to be the type of artist defined by Hiram Haydn: "To the degree a man and a classical artist believes in the essential congruence and interdependence between the ideal and empirical reality, between that which should be and that which is, to that degree does he live in the conviction that it is possible without opposition to accept the authority and discipline of an order or firm rule."[16] And how can we class among rebels this artist, monk, and courtier who, when illustrating holy books of the richest kind, based himself on old experience, the experience of others, and even copied the patterns of others?

Luckily, modern theory no longer demands one-sided explanations, such as those which hold that mannerism can easily be explained as an expression of reformatory currents, or as a Counter Reformation. At the end of the book already quoted, Eugenio Battisti, with laudable caution, called even his final conclusions "temporary in the greatest measure". Where can we place Giulio Clovio within the basic dichotomy always present in the studies of Battisti himself: classicism and anticlassicism? But are those concepts applicable to the historical actuality of the *cinquecento*? If Raphael represents the paradigm of *classical art,* do Giulio Romano and Giorgio Vasari belong to *classicism?* And finally, in which manner would this classicism, or classicism understood in such a way, be Counter-Renaissance, either from the aspect of content or of style and form? This is the question to which the "Counter-Renaissance thesis" still owes us an answer. Although Eugenio Batisti accepted it as a "provisional working hypothesis"[17], and included classicism in the general denomination at the end of his introductory speculation, when he came to theis more precise definition of that essential dualism of the *cinquecento*, he expressly stressed: "But dualism, to which we pointed in the culture of the *cinquecento,* decreases and is almost anulled only when anticlassicism manages to become predominant, almost like the devil who hangs himself on St. Michael's scales. The mannerist period is one such case."[18]

The question we come to now is: does the eliminate that first current, the current of classicism, from the concept and region of mannerism? Are we not, in other words,

thus induced to stregs more sharply the difference between classical art (in the Wölfflin sense) and classicism?

In order to avoid such artificial and ambiguous stylistic boundaries, we propose instead a polarization of a more technical nature, i.e., *imitative* versus *creative* mannerism. This determination also necessarily involves a general historical evaluation. Creative mannerism refers to a stylistically singular innovation, of a spiritual rather than academic-formal significance.[19] This category includes many excellent painters, from the early Florentine breakthrough in the second and third decades, through the Emilians, Barocci, Lilli, some Venetians including El Greco, to Lombardian and Genoese pre-baroque artists. But there is always the ever present problem, and need to evaluate it: to what degree the imitative moment or the factor of tradition (more or less always present) was elevated and overcome in that, restless and "liberated" period.

The concept of *imitative* mannerism has its roots in the polemics between Werner Weisbach and Nikolaus Pevsner[20], which were so important for the development of theory about the sixteenth century. We might be tempted to identify our polarization between *imitative* and *creative* mannerists with the polarization between classicism and anticlassicism, were it not for the fact that classicism has so many moments of creation, and anticlassicism so many of imitation. However, in the light of more recent monographic research and our insatiable "saving of values", all those black-and-white differentiations have lost their absolute valute. Our polarization between *imitative* and *creative* mannerism thus also remains firm only in a relative sense. It always demands new concrete definition and evaluation, just as the division already mentioned between classical and classicist art also demands precise identification of every stylistic phenomenon — as in the case of Giulio Romano and Giuseppe Salviati. Where and when does classicism actually start? Does it start with the very first pupils? Do pupils (which does not always also have to mean imitators) in themselves represent secondary art in Burckhardt's sense of the word, and is their work *necessarily* anticlassical? If Raphael represents the classical which grew (only in part) out of Perugino and the cartoons in the Palazzo Vecchio, and Giulio Romano represents the *classicism* deirved from that classical, this does not mean that his follower, Giulio Clovio necessarily belongs to the *anticlassicist* curent regardless of the measure in which in other ways his art is "derivatory" and secondary, even tertiary. Perhaps it would be opportune to quote here an excerpt from Hauser's introductory chapter: "Because, finally, to maintain that mannerism is anticlassical, not mentioning that it is also classicist, means not only to prejudice, but also to falsify truth. Just as it is only a half-truth to consider it antinaturalist and formalistic. Mannerism bears characteristics of the naturalistic and anti-

Adoration of the Shepherds, Windsor Castle, Royal Library

10

naturalistic, just as the rational in it is not predominant over the irrational. An acceptable concept of mannerism can only result from the tension between the classical and anticlassical, sensual and spiritual, between tradition and desire to change, convention and revolt against any kind of conformism."[21]

Here, at the beginning of his basic and detailed work, the best mannerist theoretician gave his most precise definition of the phenomenon. For Eugenio Battisti, too, classicism was an essential component of the century and permeated almost everything of value in it, but it is not completely clear whether he also considered it one of the components of mannerism.[22] Some authors single out classicism as a separate current of the century, one which lived and developed a separate life on the basis of a special artistic consciousness. But Battisti's concept of the interlinking of styles is probably much closer to the truth. This is the factor we must stress in our study of that style and that century. It is neither possible nor necessary to separate *classicism* from *mannerism* genetically and stylistically (and especially not chronologically in the sense of Sypher's "Four Stages of Renaissance Style"). They coexist and can often be found together in individual styles of that time. Nevertheless, they differ in basic aspiration, in characteristics of expression, and in spiritual motivation. In the end, the free expression of mannerism covers classicism.

We cannot deny a classicist component in Tintoretto's *Golgotha* in the Fraternity of S. Rocco, or even in his *Flight into Egypt*. But how difficult it is to find traces of it in the luminous magic of *St. Mary Magdalen* or *Mary of Egypt*. A classical, or even classicist, foundation is more than visible in Michelangelo's *Last Judgement;* the inner tension between classicism and the ruling mannerist freedom of expression was a decisive factor in the delicacy and imagination of El Greco. A classicist foundation is characteristically obvious in many of his paintings of the Virgin, but much less so in, for instance, the *Vision of the Apocalypse.* How present is the classicist foundation in Bellange, Maitre de Flore, Caron, Sprangher, Cornelis van Haarlem, or in the Francesco Studiolo in the Palazzo Vecchio? Whichever way we turn within the wide horizons of the European *cinquecento*, this tension (it would be difficult to call it contradiction) between classicist conventions in form, gesture and manner, and free expression founded on new individual observation and imagination offers scenes of miraculous diversity and, paradoxically, of unity. If *Women at the Grave* by Jacques de Bellange mark a typical possibility of transcending classicism by exaggerating its own characteristics, *Bathsheba Bathing* by Cornelis van Haarlem is sensational because of the new and imaginative observation of nature and light. Both are innovators; both are mannerists.

With the depiction of nature, a new tension appears between convention and observation, a classical foundation and a new realism, an inherited formal ideal and the reality of light and color. Works of distinct style and completely new freedom grew out of that tension. One notable painting was *Judith Showing Holofernes's Head,* by Abraham Bloemart (in the Kunsthistorisches Museum in Vienna), in which the use of color and light are superimposed upon the delicate morphology of classicism. There was also the great Northern Italian circle of Camille and Giulio Cesare Procaccini and the new realists in Lombardy: Cerano, Mazucchelli, Danielo Crespi. Nowhere else did mannerism so approximate morphologically and genetically the baroque as in the Lombardian phenomenon. This movement was long ignored by critics, as was the phenomenon of the Studiolo in Florence (1570—72). There, the cold, classical abstract line of Bronzino and Allori and their followers continued in the new realism of Masa da San Frediano, Cavalori and Macchietti. On that tension they built their own somewhat romantic painting. It is like a magic arch springing out of classicism in the middle of Florence, its first homeland. It is, in fact, one of the arches of curiosity and exploration stretching across the chasms of that diverse and critical century. Luckily, the arches crossed those chasms and carried over to our days. Modern critics noticed that "polyvalence" a long time ago; Hauser and Battisti gave it theoretical confirmation.[23]

Will Giulio Clovio find his place here?

In order to establish Giulio Clovio's place in this general ferment, on a level which explains his early fame and his later oblivion, we must have a means of distinguishing between classical art and the classicism that grew out of it. Currents of miraculous freedom and originality emerged out of that classicism, but some artists chose to develop within the closed conventions of tradition. Clovio was an artist of this kind. If classicism is the constituent and constant foundation of mannerism, perhaps the time has come to acknowledge those who preserved that foundation. Relying on tried values, avoiding the labyrinth which was becoming more and more complex, they sought support in an idealized world of form (as they also sought safety within a secure social framework). After the *sacco di Roma* chaos seemed very close. Shortly before then Giulio Clovio had faced in Hungary the threat of the Turks and the defeat at Mohač. Religious storms were already raging in Europe. In those troubled times painters faithful to the great tradition tried to preserve constant values. "For them artistic form was not essentially either a means of imitating nature or of expressing themselves, neither idealization nor stylization, but a means by which they might escape from a world that seemed to them foreign and often very suspicious, to transcend this world in some way or another, denying it or showing how much they despised it trough forms fantastically sublime or impudently unrestrained.[24]

All was on the brink of chaos: the Papacy humiliated, Florentine liberty cramped. In 1520 Luther burnt the Papal Bull, Englands was lost in 1531, in 1532 Sultan Suleiman reached Vienna, the Reformation reached Geneva in 1541. Wars raged in Germany between Charles V and Francis I. In shattered Italy only a few islands of peace remained. Giulio sought shelter from monastery to monastery, from court to court. What was to become of art in that chaotic period? What could be relied on in thought and art?

Can the immobility of the "Michelangelo of the miniature" in this tempestuous time be explained by the security of his shelter in the Farnese Palace, or by his illnesses?

He himself was probably truly at peace in his knowledge and belief, modest and withdrawn in his desires, as were many others, buoyed up by a universal spirit and style that went beyond the merely personal. But with regard to Clovio it is difficult not to call to mind the invocation Gustav Réné Hocke found in Gottfried Benn: "May the Lord preserve in them their instinct for imitation."[25]

12

In the early work there was a certain emptiness. According to Vasari, Clovio copied Dürer's engravings in Rome for his first patron, Cardinal Domenico Grimani. This makes it even more difficult to solve the problem of whether or not it was he who painted the "northern landscapes" in the Missal of Juraj of Topusko (known as the *Zagreb Codex)* made for Šimun Erdödy in Budapest between 1523—1526.[26] It is certain that his classicist education started during his first stay in Rome (from 1516 to 1523, if we presume that he went to the Eternal City as soon as he came to Italy). This was primarily but not exclusively owing to his connection with Giulio Romano. Unfortunately we do not have the fruits of those connections and thus there is an almost incredible gap of over 14 years that we are not capable of filling in (if we overlook the remaining *Windsor Folio).* Did Clovio really paint those small landscapes in Northern style in the *Zagreb Codex?* They are not easy to distinguish from those in the same missal painted by another miniaturist, which are even found on the same pages. Two regrettably lost works, *The Judgement of Paris* and *The Death of Lucretia* which, according to Vasari, Clovio painted for the king of Hungary, might have revealed more of Clovio the classicist.

Except for a small self-portrait from 1528, which is probably a copy, the first authentic (signed) work to appear after this dark period is the beautiful *Windsor Folio.* It is thought to have belonged to a choral made in about 1530 for the St. Ruffino Monastery in Mantua, or perhaps for one in Canadiana near Padua. The essential characteristics of that folio are its Venetian style, somewhat eclectic and still early-Renaissance in essence, and a successful fusion with elements of Roman mannerism. It is as if in that Venetian episode Giulio Clovio wanted a rest from the terror, death, and destruction he had witnessed in Rome. Vasari leads us to believe that this folio vas made in Candiana in cooperation with Gerolamo dei Libri, but it is so coherent (it is also signed) that we cannot be certain about that.[27] The loss of the choral makes it impossible for us to visualize the pathos and depth of that fusion of Roman classicism with fine Venetian and Veneto's realism, which in the Venetian miniature continued deep into the sixteenth century from the end of the *quattrocento.* The influence of Mantegna and Carpaccio mingle in the *Windsor Folio.* In spite of obvious eclecticism, Clovio here achieves a high level of art in a tradition that we can follow from Gerolamo da Cremona to Benedetto Bordon.

It is not easy to imagine, before that expression and that level, Giulio Clovio as the author of the landscape tondos in the *Zagreb Codex,* but it is also not easy to imagine him as the author of the *Windsor Folio* after his long mannerist experience in Rome. This folio surprises us with its firm style, but how to explain its appearance after two stays in Rome?

Is this proof of a great instability of expression?

Comparing the *Windsor Folio* with the later *Grimani Evangelistary* (1531—34), we can see the transition from the Veneto character to the Roman *gran maniera,* especially in the style and color of the illustrated scenes. The tondos with landscapes in the backgrounds remind us of those in the *Zagreb Codex,* dubitatively attributed to Clovio. The landscapes of the codex are small masterpieces, painted with a feeling for *plein-aire* and light, a direct observation of atmosphere, and an almost "impressionist" choice of subject. There is no sign of the hard *quattrocento* style of the Paduan-Venetian miniaturists, Antonios Maria Sforza or Benedetto Bordon. Only the figures in the codex, obviously done by another hand, are vividly *quattrocento* in style. The misfortune lies in the fact that the backgrounds of the miniatures painted by another hand also show some very similar landscapes, although more summary and weaker in type. Clovio's possible cryptogram on fo. 132 cannot guarantee his presence in the *Zagreb Codex.*[28]

Everything that could have been created by the young Clovio in those Roman beginnings, under the tangential influence of Dürer, who obsessed the first mannerists during the second decade, will probably continue to remain a secret and a problem for us. It is not clear to what extent he was independent in the first Roman period, and how he achieve the transformation from *imitative* classicism, following Giulio Romano, to his own expression. The *Windsor Folio* throws us into uncertainty. The Grimani Evangelistary resolves that uncertainty, presenting a synthesis of Raphaelism and Michelangelism in the frame of the Venetian *inquadratura,* of course very much purified. Is it possible that the *Windsor Folio* represents a work of cooperation between Clovio and his teacher of miniature painting, Gerolamo dei Libri, during their stay in Candiana near Padua? It is difficult to credit this theory because of the signature Clovio put on this folio, but we cannot deny the folio's eclectic openness, which indicates that Clovio was still in a stage of learning and assimilating.

Maria Cionini-Visani correctly drew attention to all the significant components. Although the impostation of initials is Venetian, with lovely interiors and Carpaccio-like figures (which, in their fullness, surpass the narrative hardness of the *quattrocento),* and although St. Theodorus looks as if he had descended from a painting by Mantegna, the three faces on the *asta* of the letter "P" display a mannerist freedom in the trace of Raphaelsque grotesque totally unknown in the Paduan-Venetian painting of the time. If he did, we must ask ourselves: where are those classicist beginnings of Clovio? Two graceful small atlantes, also painted in the mannerist fashion, hold the heavy column. The dynamics of the remaining decorations, however, are classical, with no aspiration towards paroxism. This is a moment of equilibrium in the transition of styles, lacking determined individual characteristics. This large and magnificent folio, all that has been preserved of the precious codex, greatly surpasses the production of the Paduan-Venetian circle of that period. Comparison with any work by Benedetto Bordon, early or late, in the *Dublin Evangelistary* from 1523, for instance, is enough to illustrate the imaginative superiority of Clovio, who had brought into this milieu an artistic culture that had matured in the focus of Roman High Renaissance.

The chronological relation of the folio to the *Grimani Evangelistary* in the Marciana is not clear. The proposed dating of the *Evangelistary* after 1531 is probably correct and its generally Venetian foundation is obvious. The figures of Evangelists are connected directly on the small figures in the *Windsor folio,* but they appear monumentaly and uniquely in the individuality of their faces. In some there is a slightly unskillful clash between figures and ruins in the background (as in the two of St. John, fo. 6 v and 134 r), in others figures are placed in rectangular interiors, made monumental by the simple dynamics of contours and folds (Andrew and Mark). Matthew is painted simply and intimately. The miniature showing the Evangelist Mark in an interior has a brief border of unusual chromatic harmony: cyclamen and gold. A similar classical firmness of foliate ornament had not been in that region until this time. The tondo in grisaille is a small masterpiece of High Renaissance invention, making novelty use of red, blue and gold. The concept of ornamentation on the folio showing *St. Matthew and the Angel* (fo. 52 v) in lively conversation is also new. Realistic lighting highlights the pair, while the traditional cherubs, painted with a new fullness of form and gesture, surround another skillfully painted scene in an oval. The oval on the folio of the *Adoration of the Kings* contains a cavalcade painted in gold, and there is an excellent *rocaille* in white on a gold background with the *Epiphany,* an eclectically composed scene also surrounded by *plein-aire.* The *Circumcision* is mannerist in a truly individual sense, with large "baroque" folds, while a small oval with a white head in the purple-gold ornament evokes the Venetian archaeological tradition.

With the arrival of the fourth decade it became imperative to break away from the traditional ambience of the Veneto; at least, that is how we imagine Clovio's state of mind at that moment. This was the period of transition from the *Grimani Evangelistary* to the *Stuart de Rothesay Book of Hours,* today in the British Museum (1534—38). These "paintings" (because that is what they in fact are, with deep space and lighting) are the logical continuation of those in the *Grimani Evangelistary;* the decoration of the frames is already mannerist: putti, armour, elements of the grotesque and medallions with minute scenes abound, along with small landscapes unnaturally deepened under pictures showing the main themes. This is already the peak of paradoxical accumulation, and it appeared relatively early — in the first half of the fourth decade. It is this moment that marks Clovio's move from classical harmony to the multiplicity of mannerism. The artist is feverishly searching for "lovely things" in a world of ornament and decoration. He wants to surprise and astonish.

This is now the classical as a *meraviglia.* All the elements are conventional and known, but their relations are new, and because we are talking about miniatures, everything is allowed. There are *ignudi* here, and other scenes from the Sistine ceiling, and masks familiar from the opus of Giulio Romano. The flight of space on David is purposely stressed, and perhaps this folio is the best because of the tension between frame and picture. On the much less burdened folio showing Christ on the Grave of Lazarus, this "modern" mannerist sensibility adapted the medieval theme of a struggle between a knight and a skeleton, and with a fine slant of irony set it in opposition to the theme of the resurrection. Joy and sadness are combined in the "illogical" composition. But joy always predominates, and because of this Clovio is more a classical artist than anything else. Mannerist tension is only partly present, perhaps most in this opposition and the bizarre summing up of themes on frames, inside which the painting lives its separate artistic life. Maria Cionini-Visani correctly evaluated the philosophy which underlies this eclecticism:

"Clovio makes nothing up, but consciously realizes the *regolata mescolanza* (Gilio) of elements of a culture completely absorbed, with the disinvolvement of an eclectic who fears no concubinage if its artificiality finds an impulse for technical skill and the play of intellect."[29]

However, amidst the eclecticism and accumulation of *varietas rerum* there is measure, which restrains the impulse towards chaos and the labyrinth. If mannerism, that radical game on the boundary between life and death, beauty and horror, really "destroys the theological bridge between beauty and truth"[30], then Clovio's classicism always remains on the near side of the bridge. He sustains the serene beauty of the Renaissance, and his inventory contains no enigmas or "hieroglyphics". His style is neither hermetically closed nor melancolic, unless we take its dependence upon the classical as a sign of relaxation. Clovio was not concerned with the reat problems which were posed during this era, revealing spiritual crises: in Florence during the second and third decades, and then in Rome where Michelangelo was preparing a great turing point with the *Last Judgement.* Clovio was still in Perugia under the protection of the papal nuncio Marino Grimani. In 1537 — 1538 he painted for his patron the *Commentary to the Epistles of St. Paul* (Soane Museum, London).

Both the manner and the spirit of these miniatures recall the *Book of Hours;* both are from the same complex of works of the thirties. The greater ceremoniousness of the later codex is obvious from the front page, where Clovio wrote a large inscription above the text itself, separating inscription from text by a deep landscape. He also painted the portrait of the nuncio. The imaginative dragons flanking the oval are a novelty, inventively held up in a green landscape by a group of cherubs. The *ignudi* in the upper corners continue the theme from the former codex and other motifs are also continued and varied, as we can see by slowly passing our eyes down the rich margin. The figure of Mars, attired like a Roman warrior, is also unusual. On the other side is the Parmigianino-like figure of Venus. Parmigianino's influence is withdrawn and measured, and at the same time sublimated in the Clovio manner.

This is a secondhand classicism, and thus mannerism, but there is no "sense of dread", unless we feel some emotional tension in the accumulation of armor and shields with masks. These, however, are lightened by light colors, which are a feature of Clovio's mannerist position. On the exceptional folio with the Raphaelesque *Conversion of St. Paul,* the dynamism of the frame enhances the dynamism of the motif, but the exasperation is completely artistic, formal rather than emotional — and this at a time when in Florence Pontormo was being maddened by the great difficulties of *The Last Judgement* in the choir of San Lorenzo. A drawing in the Brirish Museum repeats the theme of the conversion with greater Emilian *preziosità.* This indicates the growing influence of Parmigianino and a new stage in the development of Clovio's mannerism.

It would be interesting to consider to what extent our miniaturist was dependent on imitation in his creativity. He painted the pilaster imitating those in the Vatican Loggias on the folio with the head of Minerva, with a lush landscape at the foot, but he was not capable of composing the left pilaster, where fine details are superimposed without logical connection. On the margin of the following folio, the foliate ornaments and lovely mandorla again achieve simple, but noble unity.

Masks, festoons, and grotesques make the following codex different from the previous works. This is the *Stanzas Concerning the Eagle's Undertaking* by Eurial d'Ascoli, most probably from about 1540. Both illustrated folios suffer to a certain degree from weighty and clumsy composition, so that we experience them better in details. However, it seems that the profane subject liberated the artist's imagination. In the main scene of the allegory he created an unusual fable free of any mystic or infernal images. When we take into account the light colors, chiefly based on pale red with much gold and some blue, we find ourselves at a new stage in Clovio's creativity.[31]

The growing independence of the painting, which we have been following, reached its peak in the folios that filled Francisco dé Hollanda with admiration when he saw them in Clovio's studio (while he was still with Grimani). These are today in the Louvre, without margins: *Three Theological Virtues* and *St. Paul Blinding Elima*. All that could be distilled out of the mannerist figure-painting of Rome and Emilia he concentrated in those scenes in a measured and economical manner, adding a breath of the absolute perfection of German Renaissance realism. The figures are framed in pure classical architecture, throwing the artificially tall figures of the women and the true-to-life gestures into relief. A third folio in the Louvre is an archetypical mannerist painting. It shows *Christ Presenting the Keys to Saint Peter* before a deep Northern landscape, with classical ruins, and with gesture and mimicry elevated to maximally affected pathos. This is truly *la gran maniera* transferred to the miniature. From this point on, through to the completion of the *Officium Virginis Farnese*, Clovio must be considered a true painter in every sense. But what does this codex, Clovio's greatest work, mean in his opus, and what in the framework of that period and that style?

The codex follows the unwritten law of the Renaissance miniature, which was regarded as a "translation" and "application" of painting to another, smaller type of art. It is a reflection of Renaissance classical art, reduced of course, but attempting to remain harmonious and ideally beautiful. Arranged in pairs, the illuminations in this prayer book are, in fact, paintings that continue classical concepts, chiefly those of Raphael's circle, and some modified ideas of Michelangelo. Thus these "paintings" are still classicist in the sense in which some theoreticians determine the classical herritage, mannerist imaginative liberty had not yet swayed order and balance. We often see conventional paintings that were made to please; we would place in this category the *Annunciation, Visitation, Meeting Between Justice and Peace, Circumcision, Meeting Between Solomon and the Queen of Sheba, Coronation of Esther, Holy Family,* and even the scene of the *Crucifixion*. We recognize many borrowings, which can be justified by the rule of transcription, supposedly allowed in "in picturae minutae artibus", only confirms that miniature painting was now approaching its end announced long before. But there are pages on which this last miniaturist fully retained the classical level of harmonious composition, rendering life and freshness rarely seen in that *late time*. Such are the following scenes: *Christ's Birth Prophesied, Tiburatian Sibyl and Augustus* and *Descent of the Holy Spirit*. The *Annunciation to the Shepherds* and the *Baptism of Christ* are also exceptionally fine small "academies". When we admire the translucent bluish-green spaces that form the background in some folios (especially in the *Visitation, Meeting Between Justice and Peace, Baptism of Christ, Flight into Egypt* and *Adoration of the Magi*) we can understand why this painter of miniature anthologies, who made his home in the palace of the great cardinal, enjoyed such renown in that syncretistic period. To what extent was this circling within already known *maniere* mannerist in the modern sense of the word? Can we find traces of the instability and rebelliousness, the doubt and melancholy, and all that belongs to the night side of life and soul?

The signs of Clovio's mannerism may be found in the exasperated overabundance of decoration, especially in the frames, where trophies, masks, and grotesques are massed together. Another indication is the hypocritical balance, which amounts to conflict, between holy scenes and naked bodies shown with frank sensuality. The painter rarely bypasses the opportunity to depict, in the margins, Parmigianino-like figures of women undulating on pedestals or in niches and ephebi of idealized beauty, even beside the scene of the Crucifixion. Obviously the laws of the Counter Reformation had not yet taken hold if Clovio was able to depict, in the margins of *David in Prayer,* two nudes which seems to anticipate the refined sensibility of the *dixhuitieme*. Maria Cionini-Visani is right in stressing this richness of decoration in connection with the mannerist aspects of Clovio's art.[32]

On these folios a humanist sophistry finds connection with a very modern category of artificiality. It emerges from former art, already seen, much more than from nature; from ideas that are above the visible; from visual sensations that permeated the whole of Clovio's time and the atmosphere through which he moved. It can be seen in the archaeology and in trophy frames, in cameos and statuettes, even in landscapes (seen on countless paintings from those by Patinir and Dürer, to those by Brughel); an artificiality that tries to astonish, i. e. whose "purpose is to surprise". A new euphoric condition, surely the sign of liberation from former conventionality, emerges. We feel this erotic sublimation, as a latern desecration, often hidden, but the same often openly present in the manner of the freest Renaissance relationships.

We cannot say that Clovio has reached a stage of doubt and exploration, nor can his work yet be considered anticlassical. We see only the liberty of a courtier protected by the culture and power of patronage; liberty *a priori* limited, in profession and craft. But within these limits (and in this *Officium*) we can see signs of a nervous and neurotic condition. On the tempestuous folio showing *Uriah's Death*, the *preziosità* of the "second mannerism" and the light colors veil the cruelty of the scene; in the folio showing *The Crossing of the Red Sea*, the water spout separates the scenes in a completely anticlassical manner. Clovio is playing a clever and artifical game — there is no mannerist terror or horror. Perhaps this is what should determine Clovio's place within classicist mannerism. His paintings are gay and optimistic, academic in behavior and motivation, to be sure, but in finesse they anticipate some of best features of the Studiolo, three decades in advance.

Having located Clovio the classicist, we must now search for the tangents of anticlassicism within this stylistic framework.[33] There is no need to determine strictly the position of Clovio in that period of the hypocritica — or dual — face of mannerism (and in that period, in the classicist current of Central Italy, its hypocricy was most clearly expressed). The same contradiction can be found in his whole opus, and especially in this particular codex. Perhaps it would be more exact to ask ourselves whether it is even necessary strictly to determine the contradictions in general characteristic of this transitory period: a period of pupils and followers and of skilled masters who know and can do anything? Isn't Clovio a master of much knowledge and many possibilities, doesn't he have his place among countless patterns and paragons, but — as we have seen — just for that reason always on the brink of some new "sublimation"? These seem to emerge of their own accord, from the play of skill and imagery, without any great catharsis or disturbance. The artist's life had become tranquil, in the shelter of the large palace (and in the shelter of art). No one can say with absolute certainty in what measure *The Death of Uriah* or *The Crossing of the Red Sea* are classicist, and in what measure they are anticlassicist. In the *Adoration of the Shepherds,* which is full of borrowed elements, the fluid lighting, pink and unreal, is in a completely new category in spite of Coreggio and Bassano, and anticipating Tintoretto. This whole game, the picture of a picture, form born of form, is a sign of content and security, trust in tradition. One could imagine it was enough only to float above the models in a masterly fashion to achieve a work that would be "in the style", or on the border of the style.

The *Triumph of Death* seems to have crossed the "border", to be imbued with mannerist anxiety and derangement of the nerves. This cold, lightly colored horror of pale corpses and multicolored trophies impresses us as completely modern and unclassical; at the same time we are conscious that all those details, which impress us as morbid and terribly concentrated, have already been seen. But there is no escape from the past. Anticlassicism grows directly out of classicism (even from the classical) in shifts that are sometimes sudden and very complete in the manner of Pontormo or El Greco but often also gradual (in the manner of Proccacino or Allori).

In the same manner classicism also grew directly out of the classical ("the automatism of forms created from the spirit", wrote Hauser), which was already an "institution", characterized by an expression that was moderate and guided by certain ideals and activities; and which had had already become a form of the spirit, institutionalized and conventionalized. It seemed impossible to overcome that automatized mechanism, to emerge from the repertoire of great prototypes. "In art every style towards mannerism — like every vision of the world that inspires it — either shows traces of suffocated spontaneity and mechanized reaction, or shows signs of sustained struggle, developing exasperated forms of individuality, sensitivity, arbitrariness."[34] Clovio's expression was not rooted only in the classical and in the Farnese Palace (which in itself had become an institution), but also in the rules of a religion institutionalized to the greatest possible degree. A powerful cardinal, Clovio's patron, and the highest dignitaries of the church were already veering in the direction of Counter Reformation. The fact that the cardinal was still a champion of the Renaissance spirit was an expression of that same alienated duality that was the essence of Renaissance humanism itself. As a part of the court of Alessandro Farnese, its employee (even the horse and two servants may

be taken as a slightly ridiculous social sign of the artist's "alienation"), Giulio Clovio moved with the court to Florence after 1550(?). But his expression was already too firmly defined for Pontormo's madness in the frescoes in San Lorenzo to provoke any disorder in his vision of the world and of art. In any case, there was a great difference in function and technique, if not in genesis. An unbreachable gulf divides the peaceful piousness of Clovio (and we do not mean only the two miniatures from the Uffizi made for Cosimo Medici) from the mortified expressionism of Pontormo. Both the great teacher in the Sistine Chapel and his Florentine follower in the choir of San Lorenzo had already crossed, each in his own way, a frontier where Clovio could never follow. It was the frontier both of the classical and of classicism.

Clovio was not the only artist to stand on the edge of this gulf. The distinction between the classical and classicism found lodging in the interstices of the "heritage crisis", as I would like to call the atmosphere of pluralism in Rome after 1540 — and especially after the departure of Tibaldi to Bologna in 1553 and of Marco Pino to Naples in 1557. Because of them, the distinction becomes more and more obvious, especially when we bear in mind Pulzoni and Muziano and the appearance of Taddeo Zuccario in the Villa Giulia in 1550, and all that took place in Oratorio del Gonfalone from 1555 to 1575. Perhaps art historians have not yet clarified all the true values of the Rome of that age, but for our period the neo-Parmigianino tangents of Bertoia are too late and too sporadic, as are those of Raffaellino da Reggio. We cannot make use of them in a comparative study of Clovio. What could the Florentine milieu disclose to him? Between Pontormo's downfall and the Studiolo (1570—71) Florence was no more than a province. It nurtured a great tradition, it is true (and Bronzino's blind alley), but the thoughts of Benedetto Varci of 1546, and those of Vasari himself, were not realized in painting until the Studiolo generation; and then only in one of its lesser parts.[35]

One thing is certain: having once lost contact with Venice, and taken what he could from Emilia, Giulio withstood the pressure of the "grand manner" quite well. But the coherence of his work is no longer absolute in the second half of the century. We are no longer capable of establishing continuity, and still less of reconstructing the complete opus. Very important works from those late days are certainly four folios in the so-called Towneley Lectionary, now in the Public Library in New York (and I agree with M. Cionini-Visani and W. Smith that these date from the fifties). These are more *paintings,* with narrower frames but with the same morphology as the *Officium Farnese.* When the painter sets himself no great problems, the results are uninteresting, stereotyped scenes (*Jesus Teaching the Apostles*). But when he tries to develop the complex movement of mass in great spaces, as in *The Nativity,* we find something new. Perhaps this is where he shows his limitations, perhaps some groups are unconnected and unmotivated, but all the same, this is his effort to cross the borderline and violate convention. The illogical mases of architecture, the golden-white glory of the scattered angels create an artificial and unconvincing spectacle which is mannerist in a new sense: the scene is artificially set and acted out with no passion or flame. The *Last Judgement* is also a performance, very skillful and impassive, even naive,

Cornelius Cort (after Clovio), *Saint George Killing the Dragon,*
Florence, Uffizi, Cabinet of Drawings and Prints

and perhaps this simplicity is a measure of Clovio's originality. The gestures of the saved and the damned, the simple narratives of the inhabitants of heaven, and the connection of the lower and upper sections are all executed in an naive manner, with pale colors and diluted, fluid lighting. We understand these scenes as performances and games, without holiness and passion, but not without pathos. The pathos of gesture and mimicry, together with the light colors which in themselves negate the drama and the holiness of the illustration, make these paintings seem unstable inhabitants of the no man's land between classicism and mannerism.

The *Resurrection* from this codex shows that skill and twofold instability which is not generally characteristic only of this late period. Its fine and lightly colored sophistry make it impossible not to remember the atmosphere of the Medici Studiolo, which was just maturing; but Clovio did not yet have a feeling for its romance, nor its new colors. Nor can the feeling for it romance be found in the three miniatures from the Wildenstein Collection, which were, according to Mirelle Levi d'Ancona and Maria Cionini-Visani painted after his final return to Rome in 1565. Something of the Florentine climate can be felt in the two paintings of the *Holy Family*, but in *David and Goliath* the continuation of the *Officium Virginis* is expressively clear and firm.

Many works from this later period are missing; however, some copperplate copies of the lost works made in those years, and two works in the Sabauda Gallery in Turin (which we can attribute with some certainty to Clovio), show religious enthusiasm and pietism. The emotions of the protagonists in *The Holy Shroud* are not skillfully described; we feel none of the drama of authentic religious experience.[36] The solemn coloring is more heavy than dramatic. The composition is illogical and clumsy, markedly anticlassical in contrast to Clovio's earlier, painstaking interpretations of classical models. The folio of *The Passion*, in this same collection, is divided into four scenes which embody a much greater dramatic force, though they contain no innovations. The distinct, pale coloring highlights the emotions of the characters and allows the free flow of light.

Other than these folios, we know almost nothing of many Clovio's last active years. An evaluation of Clovio's opus, which must confirm his renown in his own time, rests on the sum of the works we have here described.

3.

The crises which shaped the history of the sixteenth century had, as we have seen, an overwhelming effect on the art of the time. Some artists overcame the alienation and ambivalence of their situation; others faded or were completely suffocated. The two greatest artists of the age, Michelangelo and El Greco, each triumphed in his own way: they were, respectively, the source and the culmination of mannerism. Michelangelo overcame the dilemma both in thought and in moral values (at the beginning of the thirties he belived that he could even escape physically by moving to Rome); El Greco first tried to realize his artistic escape from the imitative syncretism of Rome by returning to Venice; when that did not satisfy him he went even further, to the solitude of Toledo and his own characteristic expression. That, perhaps, was what enabled him to remain above the situation itself, to be its climax and emblem.

Many artists of the *cinquecento* have been forgotten over the centuries. Today art historians are rediscovering them, both the lively and the lifeless. "Polyvalent" as we are, we have already been delighted by the Lombardians of the transitory age. Federico Barocci, a great "organizer" of form and space, we perhaps still find slightly doubtful. Andrea Lillio in the Marches is about to be "discovered"; the value of Marescalchi and Venetian "late mannerist academicism" is being revealed by the Padua Institute.[37] We could add the studies of Cavalori, Macchietti, and Masa da San Friano in the Studiolo of the Palazzo Vecchio in Florence. Even better-known artists, from the first Florentines and the fabulous landscapes of Nicolo dell' Abate to the phantasmagoric scenes of Jacopo Bertoia hide many surprises waiting to be revealed. As our horizon grows wider Giulio Clovio will quite certainly not disappear, but his importance will depend on all the analysis, evaluations and the fate of this whole late Renaissance "topography".

A very unstable position, in a time unstable by definition: unstable in the degrees and forms in which it was institutionalized, and in the intertwining and inheritance of expressions. Hauser rightly stressed that the "mannerist period can be defined as a time of alienation, but also of the organization of human relations"[28]. In the case of Clovio the fact that he took refuge in security, both social and ideological, was a defense in a time of chaos, a manner of saving himself from the chasm when he was forced to move along its brink. He wanted to preserve the enchantment of beauty, the harmony he saw in great works. The institutions on which he leaned perhaps saved him from great risks and calamity, but for the same reason they separated him from life. He remained detached from the unfolding ideas and of the changes of style and expression. The danger and passionate appeal of Michelangelo's *Last Judgement* did not shake him, nor did Giulio Romano's *Gigantomachy* in Mantua (1532—1534) — not to mention other more distant "mannerist space".[39]

Thus the instabilty of Giulio Clovio was very relative; unfortunately (it must be said), because if alienation in classicism — in imitatorship of any kind, and in the syncretic combination of experience — is a *pre-supposition* of mannerism, then the revolt and subjective struggles against the seen and the learnt, the liberated morphology, are its *realization*, the true value of the new style (new styles).

When Arnold Hauser quoted that miraculous thought of Tommaso Campanello: "To comprehend means to be alienated from oneself, to be alienated from oneself means to become mad, to lose one's own identity and take on another"[40] — he did not consider alienation as falling behind (below the level of the historical moment), but as the progress of knowledge and orientation, the acceptance of discoveries. In the realm of art, however, which is in the first place a subjective and, from the point of creativity, a singular relationship, this understanding does not have that Hegelian positive aspect: in the case of nature it does not take us beyond mimesis; in the case of the comprehension of works of art and expression, it leads us only to the presupposition of an act of creation, to some kind of historical punctuality.

In the wide spaces of the *cinquecento* in Central Italy, this progress was manifested in the imitation of Raphael's models in the third and fourth decades, in the new understanding of classicism. Michelangelo's innovations inspired such artists as Sebastiano del Piombo, Marcello Venusti, Jacopino del Conte, and Marco Pino, to name only a few. The followers of Andrea del Sarto in Florence broadened the horizon with anticlassical heresies while the liberated imaginations of Emilian painters from Coreggio to Parmigianino went in another direction. The dynamic forces of the time produced many direct reactions; two of the most important were Gaudenzio Ferrari's reaction to the "classical" of Leonardo and Tintoretto's to the "classical" of Titian.

These artists were the representatives of a new spirituality. Although they sometimes consented to work within the institutionalized religious framework (we think of Tintoretto's work in the Brotherhood of S. Rocco or of El Greco's religious iconography) they remained rebellious and independent. Their modifications of style were amazingly audacious, and the power, and even purity of expression again reached the heights of Giotto, Masaccio and Michelangelo.

What, hovever, was neccessary to avoid in these speculations are absolute categories: *the classical — classicism — anticlassicism* permeate each other on their boundaries. This seems to be essential for the determination of Clovio's significance. We have already found connections between the classical and anticlassicism in Michelangelo's *Tondo Doni* and even in *David;* not to mention earlier works by Pontormo and Rosso. Coexistence and transition are usual between classicism and anticlassicism; sometimes they can hardly be noticed, but they are often very obvious. The question is whether these two phases (or modalities, or modifications) of mannerism can be antinomically posed and explained, or is it here only a question of the criteria of subjective values, and that means of creative force, when the activity of the imagination can easily assimilate a morphology found on the spot or directly passed on from teachers.

As we have said, there is no clear dividing line between *the classical, classicism,* and *anticlassicism.* They are not absolute categories, but modes of expression which overlap and coexist in the work of many artists. A skilled painter can easily assimilate a morphology, classicist or anticlassicist, that he has discovered or been taught. His creative imagination then combines the new information with other elements in a subjecitve expression, a characteristic and personal style.[41]

And if we consider this to be the relationship between classicism and anticlassicism, a relationship genetical in unity and movement, the characteristics of Giulio Clovio will be clearer and, perhaps, closer to us: his stylistic-expressional complications, and his creative range. But also his "imitations", stereotypes, and in places even his borrowings.

The circumstances of that period provide him with a double apology, if it is necessary, that can explain, if not justify, them. The first is in the character and role of the miniature at that moment. As opposed to the fantastic development and importance of painting, the miniature was a "private" and small art, almost "applied", and existed in its shadow; it was *via facti* forced to follow in the footsteps of "real" painting, even that which was monumental.

There was a certain absurdity in this, which was one of the more significant characteristics of mannerism. And Clovio began his work and lived his life among the greatest and most monumental painters. The demands of art and the taste of powerful patrons required (absurdly and paradoxically) a transfer into books of the greatness, and spirit, of the patterns even of those machless and great and spirit, of the patterns even of those matchless and greatest artists.[42] And when we imagine the role of the miniature within the general theoretic framework of classicism, and in the wake of the theories and thoughts of Pietro Bembo, Clovio's position becomes even more understandable.

He cannot be charged with "imitating only one", i. e. Bembo's already accepted point of view, confirmed in 1513 in response to Gianfrancesco Pico della Mirandola. In his achievements he was certainly much closer to the traditionalism of the Roman theoretician.[43] Even if Giulio Clovio knew about the 1512 polemic between those two, what made him take his lead from the great was the whole atmosphere, and the prestige of the great masters. Of course, he did not follo one painter alone, and Bembo would surely resent his eclecticism; nevertheless the number of those on whom he modelled himself was limited, and to be more precise, was clearly visible and recognizable. The assimilation Giulio Clovio carried out on his work is considerable, but not complete. Nor did it elevate him to the absolute spontaneity of a new style, individual and singular in history-of-art in spite of his great power of syncretism. *In style* we recognize Michelangelo, Raphael, Giulio Romano and Parmigianino. We also recognize some well-known masters *in invention.* Pico della Mirandola, however, sought completely critical and free relationship.[44] We are concerned here not with those Zeuxis's five girls of Crotone, i. e. with a relationship towards nature, not with Raphael's "idea" ("*io mi servo di certa Idea che si viene all mente*" — he wrote to Baldesiaro Castiglione); we are concerned with the possibility and the necessity for the very *maniere* of the great masters to be translated into a new modification of expression, of a relationship towards a style found on the spot, and a "learnt" one. It is certain that in his folios Giulio Clovio showed, in spite of borrowed prototypes, such a power of invention, that he obviously did not need patterns. However, patterns were needed by the miniature art of his time, and its patrons. He spend decades painting his folios in the Farnese Palace, and because of that he was limited by the demands and taste of the court, fettered by the "institution" to which he belonged. Like the fresco-decorations of high mannerism, miniature art was conditioned by the spiritual level and structure of the *milieu.* As an art "in the shadow", the means and realm of "translation into a small form", it was now doubly conditioned. Those were its last moments, but it was still strong and great because it was born in a great century.[45]

The *imagination* of the style, that basic and greatest moment of creativity, was more or less determined (even institutionalized) and worked through stereotyped invention, gestures and features. But the demand for that imagination, for a new and absolutely individual expression, did not stem from theories (nor possible "criticism") of classicism, nor from the position of the miniature, as a form of art, in classicism. It was probably too early for all the presentiments and aspirations of neo-Platonism to comprehend that antithetic and synthetic moment which opened up new epochs, that *Stilbildende Kraft,* as some German theoreticians would say. For the new epoch it was not necessary to wait for the appearance of Caravaggio. We know well that heretic declarations and liberating penetrations of style had already occurred in the wide field of anticlassicism throughout Italy and Europe: from Venice and Milan to Toledo, Fontainbleau, Haarlem and Prague. Even in Florence we have the exceptional Studiolo

episode in 1570. In Rome perhaps only Cavalier d'Arpino today again surprises us by the consequences of his consistent mannerism.

And Giulio. We must imagine him (at the end, unfortunately, very ill and old) painting on parchment in the back rooms of the Farnese Palace, ending his opus which, like a small lens, reflected part of the century. Life and art slowly constricted for him. And when they had tightened completely only Fama remained, the inconsistent goddess, and this too soon sank into darkness: Guttenberg's discovery marked the beginning of the end of the miniature. In any case Clovio's codices were destined for the darkness of libraries and treasuries and, only in these days of ours, is "Guttenberg's galaxy", greater and more powerful than ever, capable of drawing them out in a special manner (with new means) to the light of day.

Head of an Old Man,
detail fo. 92 r, Stuart de Rothesay
Book of Hours, London, British Museum

NOTES

1. G. BRIGANTI, *La Maniera Italiana,* 1961. See also L. Coletti's article in *Convivium,* 1941; R. PALLUCCHINI, "Per la Storia del Manierismo nel Veneto", *Bulletin du Musee National de Warsovie,* 1968, no. 3—4.

2. H. VOSS, *Die Malerei der Spätrennaissance in Rom und Florenz,* 1920. It was a wide panorama which showed the phenomena and their historical fate, perhaps without final definition and qualification, because it was written before there was a theoretical explanation. But it contained so many observations and ideas that it quickly provoked further research, both analyses and endeavours to synthesize. Synthetic explanations came first, and much later, after long positivistic exploration, came a new comprehension both of details and of the of the entirety of the phenomenon. Literature on mannerism, wich was rare and selected in the days of our early interest (G. GAMULIN, "Manirizam između suprotnih ocjena" Mannerism Between Contrasting Evaluations/ Izraz 102, Sarajevo 1960), has today multiplied, and it is difficult even to examine it. We shall not exploit it needlessly here, but it is necessarily included in all our research of the Renaissance, and in our thinking about it.

3. A. HAUSER, *Il Manierismo,* Italian translation, Ed. Einaudi, 1965. pp. 10, 11.

4. E. BATTISTI, "Il Concetto d'Imitazione nel Cinquecento da Raffaello a Michelangelo", *Commentari apr.* June 1956. p. 96 ff. It is interesting that, as far as is known to me, only one miniature by Clovio has been reproduced in literature on mannerism, in J. Sherman, *Mannerism,* Penguin Books, 1967, ill. 100.

5. T. KLANICZAY, *La Crisi del Rinascimento; il Manierismo,* Italian translation, Ed. Bulzoni, Rome 1973, pp. 45, 46.

6. "One could talk about a catastrophe of the spirit which preceded that of politics, and which came about because the old secular, ecclesiastical, secular-scientific and artistic dogmatic systems and categories of thought had crumbled . . . when such a world-wide construct as was that of the universe of the Late Middle Ages, Renaissance, and Reformation disintegrates there must be ruins. Artist and many others too, in all the realms of the spiritual, lose the security of those general maxims to which their persistence, ambitious goals and the small span of thought can link themselves. And thus we find ourselves faced a scene of great confusion in the many-layered mixture of the old and the new. Philosophers, writers, scientist, and politicians, and to no lesser degree artists, too, sought new supports and goals (in various streams) in many directions, artists for instance, in skillful craftsmanship or in new formulas of abstraction, which they knit into academic science and theories".
(M. DVOŘAK, *Kunstgeschichte als Geistesgeschichte,* München 1928, p. 270). In certain circles it is usual to talk scornfully about the "general"

discussions of German criticism between the wars. Doing so we forget that it was these critics, with cultural-historical breadth and with a theory that was on the absolute level of the time, who first began to examine these unexplored regions. Were they not, mostly those of the "Viennese school" (from Max Dvořak to Alfred Hauser), also the first to explain the mannerist phenomenon? That is why we quoted those reflections of Max Dvořak, from one of his old lectures (1920), which first showed the historical reasons for those shifts and changes.
His last words quoted above are applicable to Clovio and suggest the reasons which caused us to forget his so completely. Dvořak, in his *Geistgeschischte,* perhaps stressed the priority of that spiritual decline, but it was no less significant in more recent explanations, too, regardless of the extent to which social events were deterministically given first place. If we leave aside Hauser's already classical interpretation, F. ANTAL gives a fundamental social analysis of the phenomenon ("The social bachground of Italian Mannerism", *The Art Bulletin,* 1949, pp. 102—103), and so does the chapter "La Sociologia del Manierismo" in T. Klaniczay, op. cit., 1973 p. 51. This author showed some phenomena essential for the cultural and spiritual crisis, phenomena which led from Renaissance optimism to Montaigne's skepticism: the great expansion of natural-scientific experiences, which constantly found new and more difficult riddles to solve; the intergration of various kinds of knowledge, which led to contradiction and the consciousness of such contradictions; Copernicus's system which led to a new feeling of degradation, loneliness; the general crumbling of the foundations on which rested the ideology of humanism. "For Montaigne doubt is absolute; nothing is true, nothing untrue; the only certainty is the uncertainty of our judgement; and the only knowledge man possesses is un-knowledge, ignorance" (Op. cit. 1973, p. 40).

7. M. DVOŘAK, op. cit. 1928, p. 261.

8. A. HAUSER, op. cit. 1965, p. 12 ff.

9. E. BATTISTI *L'Antirinascimento,* 1962, p. 47.

10. M. DVOŘAK, op. cit. 1928, p. 275.

11. On which discussion see in E. BATTISTI, op. cit. 1956, p. 86 ff.

12. The greatest artists of the Renaissance managed to attain the highest peak of artistic achievement, the ideal of harmonious beauty. After them only pastiche, eclecticism, academism were left . . . Thus the interior laws of artistic evolution were likely to lead even the most ambitious artists of those days to a still more refined, deformed, and complicated repertoire of forms" (T. KLANICZAY, op. cit. 1973, p. p. 41, 42).

13. "A mannerist writer tries to present things not in a normal, but in an abnormal manner. More than the natural he loves that which is artifical, that which has a false glitter; he wishes to surprise, amaze, stun. But while there is only one way in which things can be shown normally, there are thousands of ways to say them artificially. And thus it is not possible to confine mannerism within a system, as people constantly tried to do. All that can result from such attempts are contradicting and contrasting systems, which stand in vain opposition to each other". (E. R. Curtius, *Letteratura Europea e Medioevo latino* 1947). We are not interested here in this oversimplified generalization (perhaps even understandable from the aspect of the history of literature), but in the thought of the presence of many systems.

14. E. BATTISTI op. cit. 1962, p. 35.

15. In that sense Wölfflin's term and the concept of classical art, as opposed to any of its renovations and derivatives, must be preserved, regardless of whether they are institutionalized by any "academy" or not. The very suffix (-ism) itself indicates the fact that this is a derived phenomenon, which may appear later in various places and with various attributes.

16. H. HAYDN, *The Counter Renaissance,* New York 1950, p. 15.

17. E. BATTISTI, op. cit. 1962, p. 378. The thesis was first suggested by W. FRIEDLANDER ("Die Entstehung des Antiklassischen Stil um 1520", Reperatorium für Kunstwissenschaft, vol. 46, 1925) on the basis of limited material, but, unlike later expansions, very lucidly.

18. E. BATTISTI, op. cit. 1962, p. 53.

19. G. GAMULIN, op. cit., 1960, and university lectures "Seventeenth and Eighteenth Century Art in Italy", Zagreb 1956.

20. "Mannerism, in its Italian origin, is a phenomenon of the late, very intellectualized humanism of a half-tired, resigned, skeptical, and blasé class of people. They made of the noble and liberal social ideal of the Renaissance exclusively a form of elegance... What is common to the great mass of mannerist painting in all lands is that which is soulless, mechanized, artificial, and formalistic... It is an art which in its essence takes on the stamp of irreligiousness" W. WEISBACH, "Gegenreformation — Manierismus — Barock", *Repertorium für Kunstwissenschaft,* 1928, pp. 23, 24). Weishach did not give up this view even in his later work: "Zum Problem des Manierismus", *Studien zur Deutschen Kunstgeschichte,* Strassburg 1934.

21. A. HAUSER, op. cit., 1965, p. 13.

22. In my opinion, the attempt to reduce the whole complex of phenomena to one abstract and historical unity is unfounded. The character of every century, and especially of the *cinquecento,* which is perhaps richer than any other in contrasts and divergence, is represented by many different measures and values, which in it take on various components. Among them mannerism is one of the most important, the determining, to put it that way but not the exclusive. Classicism is also an essential component that penetrates everywhere with more or less force, determining the face of the century, but with no characteristic exclusiveness in its presence. E. BATTISTI, op. cit., 1962, pp. 378, 379).

23. The *coro molteplice* of Italian mannerism, as Eugenio Battisti defined it, included the expressionism of Michelangelo, the first Florentine mannerists, and the Lombardians; I would also add naturalism, the chromatic luminism of the Venetians, the fantasy of Arcimbold, decorative hedonism and the "sentimental" variants of Barocci, Lilli, Vanni, and Salimbeni. But it is hardly necesary or possible to sum up all the variants in which, in Italy itself, the century's freedom of expression was manifested. The formal and chromatic daring of Lorenzo Lotto and, later, Veronese's classics is likely to embarrass us. So will Pordenono's monumentalism, the improvisations and liberties of Romanino or Altobello Meloni, the fantasies of Cambias's nocturnes and that small bizarre Circe which, in the Verona Castelvecchio, represents the unusual and little-known art of Marescalchi. There is also that deep current of early Venetian mannerism (from Medulić, Bonifazio, and Paris Bordone, to Bassano and Tintoretto which will, together with the "late mannerist academism" (R. Pallucchini) *delle sette maniere,* experience a crisis of a special kind, but which still hides many surprises. On the problem of the exclusion of the Venetian complex from the concept of mannerism see: L. COLETTI, *Convivium,* 1941; G. BRIGANTI, *Manierismo e Pellegrino Tibaldi* 1945., and *La Maniera Italiana,* 1966. NICCO FASOLA in *Venezia e Europa* 1955, S. BETTINI, "Palladio Urbanista" *Arte Veneta,* 1961.; 1961. A. HAUSER, op. cit. 1965, in the separate chapter "Review of Mannerism in Italy"; and especially R. PALLUCCHINI in *Pittura Veneziana del Cinquecento, Giovinezza del Tintoretto* 1950, "Per la Storia del Manierismo nel Veneto", *Bulletin du Musee National de Varsovie,* IX, 1968., no. 3—4, pp. 61—70,

and the lecture rich in data and new evaluations *Lineamenti del Manierismo Europeo,* Padua 1967.—1968.).

24. A. HAUSER, op. cit. 1965, p. 28.

25. G. R. HOCKE, *Die Welt als Labirint,* Ed. Rowothlt 1957, p. 12.

26. D. KNIEWALD, "*Missal of the Čazma Provost Juraj de Topusko and the Zagreb Bishop Šimun Erdödy*" ("Misal čazmanskog prepošta Jurja de Topusko i zagrebačkog biskupa Šimuna Erdödija"), Rad JAZU, Zagreb, 1940, p. 66.

27. G. VASARI, *Le Vite* ... VIII, Milano 1965, p. 117; S. SMITH, "Giulio Clovio and the Maniera di Figure Piccole", *The Art Bulletin* Sept. 1964; MARIA CIONINI VISANI, "Un Itenerario del Manierismo Italiano. Giulio Clovio", *Arte Veneta,* 1971, pp. 123, 124.

28. The problem we thus leave *in suspenso* (until the final solution of the problem of the other painter in this Missal no. 354 in the Cathedral Treasury in Zagreb) is certainly very interesting. Posed by the Zagreb scholar Dragutin Kniewald (op. cit., 1940, p. 66. ff.), it was only partly and hypothetically accepted by Ilona Berkovitz, and is also connected with the problem of the author of the gradual in Esztergom (ILONA BERKOVITZ, *A. Kassai-Graduale és a XVI századi Kassai Festészet Különlenyomat a Gerevich-Emlekkönyvböl,* Budapest 1942. pp. 77 and 86.). Dr. Kniewald also mentions, in connection with this, the opinion of the Hungarian scholar Dr. Edita Hoffmann, and in his studies proposes the connection betwen the Zagreb and Esztergom codices (D. KNIEWALD, "*Illumination and Notation of Zagreb Liturgical Manuscripts*", "*Iluminacija i Potacija Zagrebačkih Liturgijskih Rukopisa*"), Rad JAZU, Zagreb 1944, p. 80 ff.). — In any case, Clovio's stay in Budapest from 1524 to 1526 has been proved, i. e. from the Battle of Mohač (see statements by Giorgio Vasari and I. Kukuljević-Sakcinski in. D. KNIEWALD, op. cit., 1940, p. 82.), and there is also a great possibility that the cryptogram mentioned is really his. Such a reading of the cryptogram: IVLIO CLOVIC or GIVLIO GLOVIO, presupposes that Clovio had a dual Christian name even before his ordination, which Vasari states explicitly ("*ed il suo nomo al battismo fu Giorgio Julio*"). The Northern character of these truly lovely tondos from the Zagreb Missal no. 354 can be explained by already established studies of Dürer's etchings soon after his arrival in Rome in 1516 (G. VASARI, *Le Vite* ... *Vita di Giulio Clovio,* ed VII, p. 440) and also by the influence of the atmosphere on the court of Ludovik II in Budapest. If future research, or some happy find, do not confirm this hypothesis, or in some other manner fill in the void from 1516 to the *Windsor Folio,* not only the beginnings, but the whole of this first Clovio period will remain a mysterery.

29. M. CIONINI-VISANI, op. cit., 1971, p. 126.

30. G. R. HOCKE, op. cit. 1957, p. 60.

31. Taking everything into account, it seems that Clovio was still, because of his absence from Rome, somewhat late in joining the "Roman revival", where the first personage of the "second mannerism", Francesco Salviati, had been working since 1531, and Jacopino del Conte (Raphaellism plus Michelangelo) started (in 536—37) work on his first fresco in S. Giovanni Decollato. The situation in the Eternal City had changed: Giulio Romano was in Mantua, Perino del Vaga in Genoa, (until 1538). In the fourth decade Daniele da Volterra carried out his purist reduction of what then existed of Michelangelo. The return of del Vaga in 1538 strengthened the continuity and connection with the first generation. Finally, what novelty could Vasari's presence bring? There is still a certain gap in this critical Roman decade. Thus it is not unusual that Clovio's codices from this period where founded on already "known" experiences: on the composition of Raphael's school (even on some inventions of Giulio Romano), on Michelangelo's *ignudi,* on Polidoro's archeological inventory, sometimes even on the landscape of Dossi, and very often on Parmigianino-like precision. With that heritage, he was to start his greatest work, *Officium Virginis,* for his new patron Cardinal Farnese.

32. M. CIONINI-VISANI, op. cit. 1971, p. 134.

33. That question is part of the general problem of the crisis of the Renaissance, as the most profound theoretical thought has to date posed it: "For that culture the basic problem was caused by the unexpected freedom of choice between roads already known, and those still unexplored. Do we not renounce the best part of ourselves if we allow tradition to lead us too docilely? But, on the other hand, if we renounce *a priori* every example, every norm and every rule, do we not lose ourselves too much in the chaos of our own intimacy? You become aware that tradition threatens to paralyze you, but you are also aware that it can be a defense against the new that progresses with exaggerated impetus — against the new, which you feel to be, in its whole complexity, the correct rule, but also the greatest threat to life. That contradiction

holds essence of mannerism: imitating classical ideals, it escapes from the chaos of creative life, fearing to get lost in it; stressing the subjective aspect of form, searching for the arbitrary, exaggerating more and more the originality of the formal explanation of truth. Mannerism, on the other hand, expresses the fear that form could fall back with relation to the dynamics of life, and art become rigid in inert beauty." (A. HAUSER, op. cit., 1965, p. 23).

34. A. HAUSER, op. cit., 1965, p. 100.

35. G. BRIGANTI, op. cit., 1961, pp. 58, 59, 60.

36. M. CIONINI-VISANI, op. cit., 1971, p. 140.

37. R. PALLUCCHINI, "Per la Storia del Manierismo nel Veneto", 1968, *Bulletin du Musée National de Varsovie,* IX, 1968, no. 3—4, p. 73; also the lecture in Padua, op. cit., 1967/68.

38. A. HAUSER, op. cit., 1965, p. 100.

39. "The institution not only becomes incapable of opposing more and more complex and differentiated reality, but gets out of the hands of its own creators and administrators; and follows its own road, rigid, impossible to stop, as indifferent as a spectre. But its worst trait is probably the transformation of means into goals." (A. HAUSER, op. cit., 1965, p. 100).

40. T. CAMPANELLA, *Metaphysica,* Pars I, Lib. I, & I, Art. 9; quoted according to A. HAUSER, op. cit., 1965, p. 90.

41. Arnold Hauser wrote very lucidly on the parallelisms of expression in the *cinquecento,* especially about the "coexistence of classical art and classicism, and so (implicitly) of classicsm and anticlassicism" (op. cit., 1965, p. 137 ff.). It seems, however, that the theories about the *cinquecento,* i. e. about the high Renaissance, should elaborate further this last relationship, which can be shown by different values, not only in the strength of expression, but also in stylistic and morphological categories. The concept of the "simultaneous beginnings of mannerism and the baroque", of their competition in the beginning, is neither happy nor historically-genetically correct. The birth and beginnings of the baroque were of a completely different historical and stylistic character. It is not a case here of "birth from the inside", or of the development of the same morphological bases, but of a break and revolutionary change of attitude

to nature. One can in the beginning talk about realism and a completely new relationship towards nature and the object. This turning point was, as first, connected with the appearance of a strong personality, Caravaggio, but essentially we feel here the maturing of a new social and ideological situation. Thus that sudden explosion of the new expression, Caravaggism, at first. But soon baroque realism became a general, but exceptionally diverse mark of the whole seventeenth century.

42. See also W. SMITH, "Giulio Clovio and the Maniera di Figure picolle", *The Art Bulletin,* Sept. 1964, p. 395.

43. This letter was published in Basel in 1518, but the written polemic itself between Bembo and Pico took place in 1512. It is not clear how long its echo reverberated, and in which way. If the views of G. F. Pico della Mirandola are "hostile to every principle of imitation" (*ostili ad ogni principio d'imitazione*), it is difficult to be able to consider him a theoretical representative, or at least a predecessor, of mannerism, because that style cannot be imagined (in Italy) without classicism. But the constant spontaneous process of assimilation, and the idea as a "rule of the independence of art of outside experiences" and as the "instinctive criterion of choice", is really closer to the motivations and acts of that "spiritualized mannerism", which had already overcome the stage of imitatorship and eclecticism. The *De Imitatione* letters, although written too early (at the very beginning of the century) to precisely reflect the fate and ranges of mannerism, still mark its basic polarization (data and quotations from E. BATTISTI, op. cit., 1956, sect. II and IV; see also G. SANTANGELO, "Le Epistole *De Imitatione* de G. F. Pico della Mirandola e di Pietro Bembo", *Nuova Collezione di Testa Umanistici Inediti o Rari,* XI, Florence 1954; G. Santangelo, *Il Bembo Critico e il Principio d'Imitazione,* Florence, 1950).

44. "*Inventio enim tua laudatur magis, cum genuina est magis, et libera.*" G. F. PICO DELLA Mirandola (in G. Santangelo, op. cit., p. 30).

45. Even from those several preserved letters written in 1560 to his patron the position in which he was placed can clearly be seen. From the letter, for instance, to Cardinal Farnese from Corregio to Rome (1568): "*Apresso ricardo a V. A. III*mo *che sono hormai cinque mesi che non ho avuto un soldo de la provisione che la bontà e nobilità sua mi dona . . . Ma a me bisogna qual che denari si per medici e medicine. Come anche fra altre cose accorrenti al viver mio.*" (A. RONCHINI, *Atti e memoriali,* Ser. III, 262, according to J. U. T. BRADLEY op. cit., 1891, p. 383).

Christ Crowned with Thorns,
detail fo. 166 r, Stuart de Rothesay Book
of Hours, London, British Museum

GIULIO CLOVIO

Maria Cionini–Visani

The art of the miniature reached its climax in the sixteenth century, in the work of Don Giulio Clovio. He altered the traditional forms and spirit of the art, inventing a sumptuous and frail style. The greatest of miniaturists was also the last; his was the final statement, signalling the end of the epoch of the miniature.

Clovio was a courtier, dear to princes, and a friend of artists and men of letters, a representative of the learned and aristocratic class. His work excited great enthusiasm among his contemporaries, who listed his name beside those of the greatest painters of the High Renaissance. Vasari wrote of him, "there has never been, nor will there be for many centuries either a more rare or more excellent miniaturist or, it's better to say, painter of things in little, than Don Giulio Clovio, as he has exceeded all the others who have ever practiced this manner of painting" Vasari called him "the new and little Michelangelo"[1]; Paolo Pino mentioned "Don Giulio miniaturist" among the skillful painters" of his time[2]; Borghini affirms that "in this manner of little figures Don Giulio has been most excellent"[3]. In a list which includes Michelangelo and Raphael, Leonardo and Giorgione, Lomazzo remembers "the manner of the great miniaturist Don Giulio Clovio who made it shine equally as to painting"[4]. Later on the admiration and won-

der which his work aroused in all who went to Rome is reported by Mancini[5] and Baglione[6], until Lanzi, according to whom "because of Giulio art in all Lombardy improved, in Lombardy- which to him included part of the present day Venetia"[7]. Perhaps the greatest homage was El Greco's portrait of Clovio in the *Expulsion from the Temple* (Minneapolis), beside those of Titian, Michelangelo, and another who is most likely Raphael.[8]

All the same, the generous praise of his contemporaries, which we must certainly consider to be sincere, contains a negative critical judgement in our eyes; this talk of a "little Michelangelo" and the "shine equal to the shine of painting" already reduces the status of the artist to that of a scrupulous follower of great painters and his "virtue" to the extraordinary ability of one who knew how to reproduce in a minimum size what Michelangelo and others did in the "grand manner". Shortly afterwards si-

lence fell on the miniature in general, by this time already considered *arte minore,* and on Clovio in particular.

In the nineteenth centery the miniaturist's name reappeared in art historiography. Baldinucci[9] and De Boni[10], and later on between the end of the nineteenth century and the first decade of this century, Sakcin[11], and Bradley[12], Bessone Aureli[13], Bonnard[14], and Bacotich[15] all tried, in works of a not too strict philological-critical strain, to reevaluate the figure of Clovio. Only Hebèrt reduced him to nothing more than a simple craftsman with great tehnical ability, a "servile imitator of Michelangelo and Raphael"[16]. On the other hand, the analyses of the critics of the last few years, Bye[17], Levi D'Ancona[18], and Smith[19] are well-balanced and philologically attentive; these latter place Clovio's art within the ambit of mannerism. In fact it is only possible to reacquire a taste for Clovio in the light of new historical perspective on mannerism. It is certain that

Clovio studied Michelangelo and Raphael and many others, but never academically. He mixed their languages according to the demands of a fiery imagination. In his elaborately wrought ornamentation we find the traces of his Eastern heritage, which brought him to seek in art the temporary abandonment of a restless spirituality.

Notwithstanding the exceptional wealth and interest of the documentary material in our possesion[20], it is difficult to establish what Clovio's beginnings were. Born in 1478 in the small village of Grižane, Croatia, Juraj Klovičić[21] (it was only later that he Italianized his surname, and called himself Giulio, probably in honor of Giulio Romano) he went to Venice in 1516 and was taken in by the family of Cardinal Domenico Grimani[22]. At the time Domenico lived in Rome. A keen collector of ancient works and a refined judge of contemporary art, he possessed one of the most celebrated collections in Europe. This was later transferred to Venice in 1523 according to the stipulations of his will, which left the objects of large dimensions to the Republic of Venice and the smaller ones to his nephew, the Patriarch of Venice. He and the other members of the Grimani family, Vettore (the Procurator of St. Mark *de supra*) and Giovani (the bishop of Ceneda and Patriarch of Aqulieia), continued to extend protection to the numerous artists of Central Italy who flocked to Venice.[23] In this environment between Venice and Rome, the young Clovio came into contact with early mannerism. According to Vasari's account[24] Clovio was already in Rome by 1516, working on pen drawings for coins and medals for Cardinal Grimani and copyng engravings. One of his first miniatures must have been of the *Epitome in Divaepartenices Mariae Historiarum* by Albrecht Dürer. Edited in Nuremberg in 1511, it was at that time most likely in Domenico Grimani's library in Rome. This fact is only useful

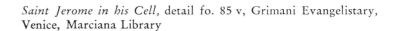

if it helps us to realize that these must have been years of apprenticeship and training for our artist, who was to return to Venice in about 1523. This training based on Dürer's prints developed the agile and robust quality of Clovio's drawing. From Venice he left for Buda, where he had been invited by Ludvig II of Hungary. He arrived with an introduction from Alberto of Carpi for whom, according to Vasari, Clovio had painted *a Judgement of*

Paris and a *Death of Lucretis.* These were not real miniatures but instead small compositions on separate sheets in "tempera and gum". This medium was often used for illustrations of a profane character destined for the private rooms, while the miniature, in the traditional meaning, was reserved for religious books[25].

In 1526 the Turks defeated the Hungarians at Mohač, Clovio escaped death by fleeing to Rome, this time in the

The Holy Evangelist,
detail fo. 133 v, Grimani Evangelistary,
Venice, Marciana Library

Saint John the Evangelist
detail fo. 102 r, Grimani Evangelistary, Venice,
Marciana Library

Saint John the Evangelist
detail fo. 134 r, Grimani Evangelistary, Venice,
Marciana Library

service of Cardinal Laurenzio Campeggio for whom he did a *Madonna di Minjo*. He also started to draw "trying with all his power to imitate the works of Michelangelo".[26] In Rome Clovio again encountered Giulio Romano who had previously advised him to paint small compositions or, better, big compositions on a small scale. Romano "before any other" had taught him "the use of dyes and colors prepared with gum and in tempera"[27]. There are even examples of small independent paintings by Giulio Romano himself (e. g. the *Madonna* at the Louvre, which measures 288 × 250 mm., most likely painted in 1516) which were called *da gabinetto*.[28] Clovio's first formation was not therefore as a miniaturist in the strict sense, but as a painter, since Giulio was his first master. None of Clovio's historiographers except Smith have given sufficient stress to such a precise piece of information.

Saint Andrew,
detail fo. 118 r, Grimani Evangelistary,
Venice, Marciana Library

Clovio's modification of the traditional miniature form is largely owed to this early training. He was, after all, a painter of his time, completely immersed in the living culture of Rome and mannerism. He drew his inspiration from the ancient and the modern alike. One of the most unusual facets of Clovio's language is his use of picturesque and grotesque motifs inspired by the rhythmic and sumptuous sequences of the Vatican Loggias. All the same, the confirmation of this formation will only be found in his later works, as no examples from this early period remain.

The fury let loose by the Landsknechts (mercenary soldiers) in 1527 and the horrors of the sacking of Rome interrupted the Sistine studies and the habits of Giulio Romano; like many other unfortunate inhabitants of Rome, Clovio suffered plunder and imprisonment. The misery of such an experience drove him to vow that if he survived he would renounce the wordly life and pass the rest of his days in a monastery. In fact, a few months later we find him a monk in Mantua, in the Monastery of San Ruffino of the Scopertino order. He registered as Giulio, after his friend who was also in the city of the Gonzagas, employed in the Te Palace. There they renewed their old friendshio. Their exchange of ideas, born out of the loneliness of exiles and artists, provided points of departure for flights of bizzare fantasy in their work.

Saint John the Evangelist,
detail fo. 97 v, Grimani Evangelistary,
Venice, Marciana Library

Clovio spent three years at San Ruffino; his face must have been melancholy and sensitive as it appears in a small miniature (formerly in the Ambras Castle and now in the Kunsthistorisches Museum in Vienna), which is encircled by the inscription "*Julius Clovius Croatus sui ipsius effigiatur A: aetatis 30 salut. 1528*". The miniature repeats court iconography as proposed by Holbein and later established by Clouet. The artist is shown in ecclesiastic garments and biretta, with a dog at his shoulder, perhaps, following the taste for allegory at that time in fashion, as an emblem of faithfulnes and devotion towards the patron for whom the work was destined[29]. The pale, nervous, and slender hand which comes out of the black garment, and the unstable and restless expression show a man who has not found freedom from the ambition of the intellectual and courtier. He is not content in the monastery even though he had seriously sought it after the anguish of that moment of danger. The long eye, the strong nose and che-

Saint Mark,
detail fo. 96 r, Grimani Evangelistary,
Venice, Marciana Library

Annunciation,
fo. 13 v, Stuart de Rothesay Book of Hours, London, British Museum

Madonna and Child
fo. 14 r, Stuart de Rothesay Book of Hours, London, British Museum

ekbones, the small thin mouth, and the blond beard, all suggest this is indeed that face of the painter. All the same, it was not his hand which painted this delicate miniature. The Flemish style of the miniature recalls the work of an artist of the circle of Sir Anthonis Mor — if not Mor himself, who was in Rome between 1550 and 1551 and could have seen a prototype of Clovio[30] from which it is most likely the portrait derives.

A large sheet signed *D. Julio Clovio F.* from Consul Smith's collection now in the Royal Library at Windsor[31]

is thought to have come from the book of anthems carried out for the Monastery of San Ruffino or that of Candiana. Both books are deteable about 1530 and were later dispersed. The page is composed in the severe style of the late *quattrocento* which required it to be arranged within the precise symmetry of a candelabrum. It is decorated with an extraordinary mixture of Venetian and Roman motifs.

It is unlikely that Clovio isolated himself completely while at Mantua or at the Monastery of Candiana (Padua) where he was transferred about 1530. He must have come

David Praying,
fo. 91 v, Stuart de Rothesay Book of Hours, London, British Museum

Head of an Old Man,
fo. 92 r, Stuart de Rothesay Book of Hours, London, British Museum

out frequently to meet artists and explore the treasures of Venice and the mainland.

He surely knew the work of Benedetto Bordon, the premier miniaturist of the early 1500's (died 1539). Bordon prolonged the *quattrocento* style, particulary that of Mantegna and Bellini. His coarsely cordial prose was very different from the agitated and restless style of his contemporary Paduans, Gerolamo da Cremona and Liberale da Verona. Bordon did not employ the common motifs derived from Cima da Conegliano, the *Mariegole* and from

the *Libri dogali* which were carried out in Venice, where nevertheless a real continuity in the field of the miniature was lacking.[32] The very fame of the Florentine Iacapo del Giallo, who wearily repeated motifs of Central Italy in the *Book of Psalms* for San Giorgio Maggiore (cor. 12 A), underlines the total lack of other more meritable artists.

The importance of Clovio's meeting with Gerolamo dei Libri which, according to Vasari[33], took place about 1530 at Candiana, should not be underestimated. Even if it cannot be considered a determining factor in Clovio's mature,

Christ at Lazarus' Tomb,
fo. 119 v, Stuart de Rothesay Book of Hours, London, British Museum

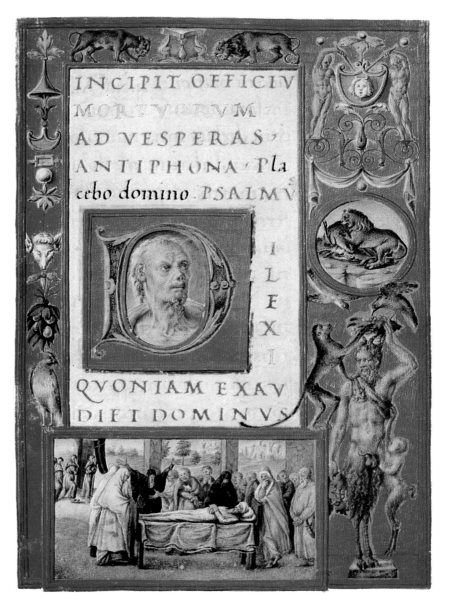

The Head of Lazarus,
fo. 120 r, Stuart de Rothesay Book of Hours, London, British Museum

romano style, it is certain that he gained greater ability and technical ease from his studies with the Veronese master. He realized that the limits of the refined art of the miniature could become the stimuli to a fanciful inspiration; it was at this moment that Clovio chose the miniature as his medium. Maybe the sober Mantegna colors of the page at Windsor Castle (for example, the frieze embellishment on the upper margin), the love of realistic detail, the sharp tones and blendings derive from the presence of Gerolamo. All the same, the vigorous coloring, so warm and dense, so

rare in Clovio's work, bears traces of the influence of Benedetto Bordon. The details: the little still life of the scissors and inkwell on the green table, the red cardinal's hat, hanging up, to underline the dignity and cordiality of the person; the bed curtains wound around the bedpost; the portrait-like treatment of the young armed page and the same domestic detail of the dog in the foreground all belong to the Venetian world of Carpaccio and Lotto. The standing figure of St. Theodore, dressed as a knight in classical armor, and the Roman bust on the architrave

32

The Crucifixion,
fo. 165 v, Stuart de Rothesay Book of Hours, London, British Museum

Christ Crowned with Thorns,
fo. 166 r, Stuart de Rothesay Book of Hours, London, British Museum

belong to Mantegnaesque humanism. The *mise en page* of the rooms is Belliniesque — a compromise between Renaissance frame and lively movement of characters, restriction and freedom. Only the slim Victory and the little Cupid which complete the ring of the "p" derive from nostalgia for the Eternal City: the wonderful pole made of leaves and masks with slanting eyes and toothless mouths that twist in a violent and unusual characterization are of the type in drawings by Pippi[34] and the profile of Minerva in the little tondo of the candelabrum suggests

the School of Raphael. It is on the whole a more Venetian than Roman sheet, belonging too much to the North of Italy to think of it being illustrated by an artist who had received his first stimulus from Giulio Romano. If we cannot imagine Clovio having conceived and executed this work independently, we might speculate that Gerolamo dei Libri was his collaborator as well as his teacher. Gerolamo could have laid out the decoration of the page, which Clovio then finished and signed. Clovio soon returned to the world; the monks were replaced by a more generous

33

Fo. 1, Commentary on the Epistle of Saint Paul to the Romans, London, Soane Museum

Page, Commentary on the Epistle of Saint Paul to the Romans, London, Soane Museum

and educated patron, one who encouraged artistic innovation and experiment. Cardinal Marino Grimani not only obtained permission from the Pope for the Croatian to leave the monastery (after Clovio, who had had trouble with a leg, had complained of the distracted treatment given to him), but also commissioned the decoration of an *Evangelistary*[35], in which the Roman and Venetian worlds again coexist. It is not easy to identify Clovio as the author of the miniature of the *Evangelistary* Codex at the Marciana Library in Venice unless his double education

is taken into account. During these years he studied the Venetian artists Vasari remembers some copies of Titian done during his years at San Ruffino) and lived in contact with Roman artists, refugees from the storming of Rome, as well as with Cardinal Grimani, who played such an important role in the introduction of the style of Central Italy into Venice.

The codex is dated 1528, but it is possible that only the text was completed at that date. The illustrations may have been added between 1531 and 1534. Except for some minor illustrations of a more modest tone for which we can consider a collaborator, I believe the decoration of the Codex at the Marciana[36] to be the work of Clovio. One can speak of the Venetian tradition in some compositions (fo. 1r; fo. 5r; fo. 6r; fo. 52v; fo. 85v; fo. 96r; fo. 102r; fo. 118v fo. 133r) in the regular layout the deep and warm tonal coloring for certain landscape openings. It is also true that in these same folios new motifs appear: the Michelangelesque cut of the figure of *St. Mark* (fo. 96r), that of *St. Andrew* (fo. 118v), the intense Dürer-like face of the same *St. Mark* and the strong dissonances of color in the scene of *St. Matthew and the Angel* (fo. 52v) which all the same maintains a Venetian and Veronese flavor in the background. The Renaissance frame with robust putti holding up a *grisaille* medallion recalls the Roman style of Perin del Vaga. The Romanism blends with the deformed accents of Northen ancestry (the study of Dürer had been intensified during these years of ethusiasm for the German master[37]) as in the scene of the *Circumcision* (fo. 9v), where the color falls harhly to cut out the pointed faces, presses the garments into great folds, and squashes the figures in a receding and tottering perspective.

Fo. 9, Commentary on the Epistle of Saint Paul to the Romans,
London, Soane Museum

35

The Madonna who vibrantly cuts the narrative content of the *Adoration of the Kings* (fo. 10v) is a reminder of Francesco Salviati.[38] Even if one does not agree with J. V. Bradley[39] that Salviati was Clovio's pupil, one cannot all the same ignore (as J. Cheney[40] briefly points out) the signs of influence between the two artists during the years in which one was illustrating the *Officium Farnese* (1543—46) and the other was painting the frescoes of the Oratory of San Giovanni Decollato, Rome (1538) and in the Grimani Palace, Venice (1539—41). It is likely that the two

more markedly Roman compositions in the *Evangelistary*, the *Circumcision* and the *Adoration of the Kings*, were added during these years. By this time Clovio's *venetismo* of 1530 had been modified by new experiences, combining in the coherent development of his mature style.

Between 1532 and 1534 Clovio traveled to Perugia, where Cardinal Grimani was papal nuncio.[41] A codex dated 1533 (City Library, Treviso), decorated and probably written by Clovio[42], is practically an *ex voto* offering following the recovery from the disturbance of his leg. A

The Conversion of Saint Paul,
fo. 8 v, Commentary on the Epistle of Saint Paul to the Romans, London,
Soane Museum

small and precious *Book of Hours,* now in the British Museum, London[43], also probably dates from Clovio's years in Perugia, between 1534 and 1538. This work can be considered a link between the *Grimani Evengelistary* and the *Commentary* at the Soane Museum.

The illustrations of the *Grimani* codex are still more or less miniatures in the traditional sense. Although they contain much that is innovative, they serve primarily as ornamentations of the text. In the Soane *Commentary* Clovio is concerned only with composing real and propor-tioned paintings on the large pieces of parchment. In the *Stuart de Rothesay Book of Hours* or *Officium,* in the British Museum, we find both types of composition, as well as a new maturity. Clovio's style breaks out rich and full, free from uncertainties and snares, as in the scene of the *Annunciation* (fo. 13v), which dissolves in delicate and blending colors, memories of the tonalism of the Veneto. The tasteful forms of domestic simplicity are surrounded by a copious frieze of arabesques, grotesques, and robust putti holding up the tondo with the *Nativity.* Roman-

styled trophies of armor surround *David Praying* (fo. 91v) and the vignette below, derived from the Sistine fresco of *David and Goliath* is a marvel of manneristic composition in the diagonal impetus of the two bodies in the foreground. Nearly identical copies of the candelabra of the Raphael Loggias decorate the scene with *Christ at Lazarus' Tomb* (fo. 119v), against a background of a Bramantesque city (this scene is a precise anticipation of *Christ and the Adulteress* of the later *Towneley Lectionary*). The vignette of the *Battle Between Skeletons and Knights* underneath is derived, through Dürer, from Martin Wolgemut. Its refinement seems to heighten rather than diminish the energy of the slim lines in the thrust of the infinitesimal figures.

The Crufixion (fo. 165), is moving and simple in the landscape. The naturalistic details in the foreground contrast with the elaborate abundance of slim and grotesque candelabra in the margins. The composition aspires to a Northern harmony of monochromes, following the example of Schongauer and Dürer in the *piè de page* (fo. 165v, 166r).

Allegory of the Catholic Faith,
fo. 1 v, Eurialo d'Ascoli's Stanzas, Vienna, Albertina Library

Tittle of the Work,
Eurialo d'Ascoli's Stanzas, Vienna, Albertina Library

The three sheets of the *Commentary on the Epistle of St. Paul*[44] in the Soane Museum, London, were painted by Clovio for his patron either during his stay in Perugia or shortly after in Rome. Here the homage to Raphael is complete, though enlivened by tension and deformation. The splendid anthology of Italianate motifs in the Soane pages is the work of an artist who invents nothing, but consciously carries out the "regulated blending" of an absorbed culture to the point of saturation. No union is feared as long as the artist discovers in the "refinement" the stimulus for technical vigor and the play of the intellect. This eclecticism carried to its furthest limits is proof of the end of the miniature as an art in its own right and its complete submission to the "nobler" art of painting.

This derivative aspect of mannerism, art feeding on itself, should not be condemned as mere manipulation or imitation[45]. The *Conversion of St. Paul*, (fo. 8v) certainly derives from Raphael's cartoon for the tapestry of the Vatican gallery, but it is also proof of Clovio's validity as a representative of mature mannerism. He transforms the

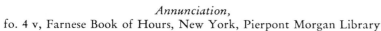

Annunciation,
fo. 4 v, Farnese Book of Hours, New York, Pierpont Morgan Library

The Prophecy of the Birth of Christ to King Achaz,
fo. 5, Farnese Book of Hours, New York, Pierpont Morgan Library

essentially balanced, Renaissance scene which the *Maestro* had drawn twenty years before; the perspective and anatomy became disproportionate, elements are added and subtracted. The figures of the main scene are poised in a precariously balanced symmetry of harmony and counterpoint. Their theatrical gestures emphasize the dazzle of unexpected chromatic harmonies. The medallion underneath repeats in minute proportions Giulio Romano's painting for the Church of San Stefano in Genoa, while the little oval miniature on the left side of *St. Paul's Ser-*

mon derives from Raphael's cartoon of the *Sacrifice to Lystra*. The list of borrowings could continue: from the Sistine nudes that twist in the top corners of the page to the border of the right-hand margin which repeats, step by step, on the pilasters of the Vatican Loggias, to the cameo of the *Three Graces* from Chantilly on the opposite side. The Roman warrior at the bottom right and the lovely head of Minerva[46] belong to the archeological repertory of Giulio Romano and of Polidoro. The animals recall Giovanni da Udine, while in the minute landscape at the *pié*

The Visitation,
fo. 17 v, Farnese Book of Hours, New York, Pierpont Morgan Library

Justice and Peace Embracing,
fo. 18, Farnese Book of Hours, New York, Pierpont Morgan Library

de page ships and figures are lost in the bluish distances of a landscape in the Dossi tradition, the ethereal colors of which evoke Patinir. Finally, the allusive eroticism of the Venus-Peace, which corresponds to the figure of Mars-War on folio 9, reminds us of "the drawings he did from Parmigiano when he was with Cardinal Grimani," listed in the inventory of Clovio's property.

The subject of the *Conversion of St. Paul* — dear to the devout sensibility of the Counter Reformation—was copied by numerous engravers of Clovio.[47] They were more inspired by a different version of the theme than by the

Soane miniature. Only a beautiful drawing in ink and water-color at the British Museum remains of that version; it is also worth mentioning the faithful copy in color which belongs to the Pinacoteca Ambrosiana of Milan, both because it is little known and also because it needs an explanation. The guide of the Pinacoteca[48] attributes it to the hand of Clovio, ignoring the words in the bottom right-hand corner which say *"Don Iulio Clovio inv. Spranghers pinxit."* This Flemish artist "who worked as a catalyzer between the various Europen courts"[49] was in Rome and at the Farnese Palace from 1567 until 1575. During this

44

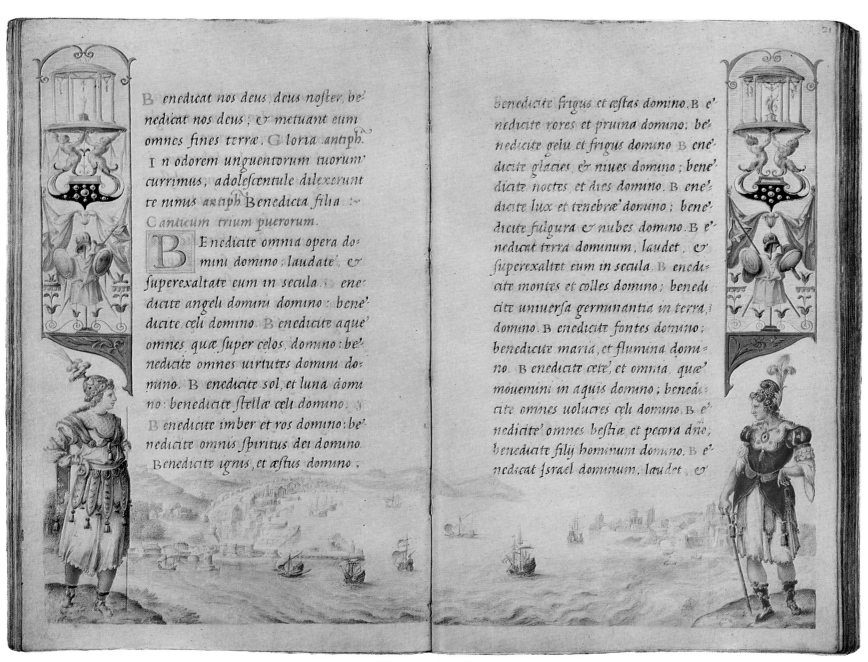

Benedicat nos deus, deus noster, benedicat nos deus; & metuant eum omnes fines terræ. Gloria antiph. In odorem unguentorum tuorum currimus, adolescentule dilexerunt te nimis antiph. Benedicta filia Canticum trium puerorum.

Benedicite omnia opera domini domino; laudate, & superexaltate eum in secula. enedicite angeli domini domino; benedicite celi domino. Benedicite aque omnes quæ super celos, domino; benedicite omnes virtutes domini domino. Benedicite sol, et luna domino; benedicite stellæ celi domino. Benedicite imber et ros domino; benedicite omnis spiritus dei domino. Benedicite ignis, et æstus domino;

benedicite frigus et æstas domino. Benedicite rores et pruina domino; benedicite gelu et frigus domino. Benedicite glacies, & nives domino; benedicite noctes, et dies domino. Benedicite lux et tenebræ domino; benedicite fulgura & nubes domino. Benedicat terra dominum, laudet, & superexaltet eum in secula. Benedicite montes et colles domino; benedicite universa germinantia in terra, domino. Benedicite fontes domino; benedicite maria, et flumina domino. Benedicite cete, et omnia, quæ moventur in aquis domino; benedicite omnes volucres celi domino. Benedicite omnes bestiæ et pecora dño, benedicite filij hominum domino. Benedicat israel dominum; laudet, &

The Bay of Naples,
fo. 20 v and 21, Farnese Book of Hours, New York, Pierpont Morgan
Library

45

Adoration of the Shepherds,
fo. 26 v, Farnese Book of Hours, New York, Pierpont Morgan Library

Temptation,
fo. 27, Farnese Book of Hours, New York, Pierpont Morgan Library

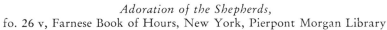

period he met Clovio, who was immersed in the courtly and pietistic environment of his patron. The Milanese copy is proof of his admiration of Clovio. The composition of the London drawing (British Museum no. 1946-7-12-322) is based on opposing and receding diagonals. The group of rearing horses and the dazzled saint are linked together by the soldier balanced on one foot with his hand extended towards Saint Paul and the fleeing horse. This scene recalls the Michelangelesque prototype of the Paoline, using the same diagonal as in the divine group in the heavens. The

tension in Sprangher's copy relaxes into softness, and the original pathos, maybe because of the weakening of the light and acidulous colors in the foamy distances of the landscape, becomes more insistent and ambiguous.

To the fourth decade and the years spent in Perugia belongs another of Clovio's works, the illustration of the *Stanzas on the Venture of Aquila*[50] by Euralio d'Ascoli. The religious, spiritual side of Clovio's nature is here overshadowed by his laical, courtesan character, which reveals itself in the exquisite elaboration of the heraldic-allego-

The Annunciation to the Shepherds,
fo. 30 v, Farnese Book of Hours, New York, Pierpont Morgan Library

The Prophecy of the Birth of Christ to the Emperor Augustus,
fo. 31, Farnese Book of Hours, New York, Pierpont Morgan Library

rical theme. A new fragility, characteristic of the period between Parmigianino and Perin del Vaga, supplants the usual tribute to Michelangelo and Raphael. Feminine warriors of equivocal grace are placed against the architectonic backgrounds inspired by Bramante and Serlio, a feature of Clovio's painting since the Stuart de Rothesay codex. The tender nude body of Faith is placed in pleasing contrast with the hard talons of the eagle. Charity, in the bottom right-hand corner, is Emilian in her pose and features, as is the female figure in folio 2, whose raised mantle becomes

an aureole, a symbol of the influence of Parmigianino. This is Clovio's most obvious homage to the Emilian painter; one could speculate that it was executed at a later date, when Clovio's relations with the Farnese and thus with the court of Parma were more frequent. Clovio did not journey to Parma until 1556[51] but he certainly came into contact with Emilian mannerism long before, meeting Parmigianino in Rome in 1527. More than any direct influence, it was the profane theme, unconstricted by iconic and devotional demands a sacred subject, which induced Clovio to choose

47

The Circumcision,
fo. 34 v, Farnese Book of Hours, New York, Pierpont Morgan Library

The Baptism of Christ,
fo. 35, Farnese Book of Hours, New York, Pierpont Morgan Library

from his "anthology" the motifs suggested by an artist who had revealed the laic and even satanic aspect of mannerism far more than the pius one. In 1538—39 Clovio was in Rome again as a guest of the Grimani, according to Francisco dé Hollanda, who went to visit him. Among the works of Don Giulio he saw a *Ganymede,* a *Venus* and two large sheets which he praised highly[52]. We do not have the miniature with *Ganymede,* to which a charcoal drawing at Windsor Castle (no. 457). presumably refers. Another copy from Michelangelo, that of *Tizio* (no. 459),

the original of which belongs to the same collection[53], derives from the drawings which Michelangelo had given to Tommaso Cavalieri[54] at the end of 1532. To him these drawings must have been examples of refinement and technical ability (with how much diligence he repeats the soft greys and the delicate sketches of the style formed in admiration of the *Maestro,* open and freed from the minutiae of the miniaturist.) Certainly he felt the suggestion of the cultured allegorical language: Ganymede, the ecstasy of platonic love, and Tizio, the agony of sensual passion.

Adoration of the Kings,
fo. 38 v, Farnese Book of Hours, New York, Pierpont Morgan Library

The Meeting Between King Solomon and the Queen of Sheba,
fo. 39, Farnese Book of Hours, New York, Pierpont Morgan Library

The large sheets which Francisco mentions[55] are very like those of the Soane *Commentary*, especially *Saint Paul Blinding Elima* (a tribute to the Raphael tapestry of the same subject), and *The Theological Virtues*. Both of the scenes, which unravel according to Raphael's balanced context of Renaissance architecture and controlled typologies, have motifs originating from Michelangelo (the *Charity* deriving from the Bruges Madonna) or from the Germans (one can see the splendid old man dressed in furs — probably a portrait — to the right of the scene of *Saint Paul*). Clovio's fantasy exults in the orchestration of unrestrained color against the rosy-grey architecture: the greens clash and the very pale yellows light up in unexpected violets, the violets in their turn change into pink, which is immediately poisoned by yellow; the gold is bordered with block, and the faded red of the cap becomes purple in the trousers of the page. The clear, hard tone of lapis-lazuli dominates over all, a light shining without warming, lending no weight to the incorporeal, dazzlingly colored objects in the tableau.

49

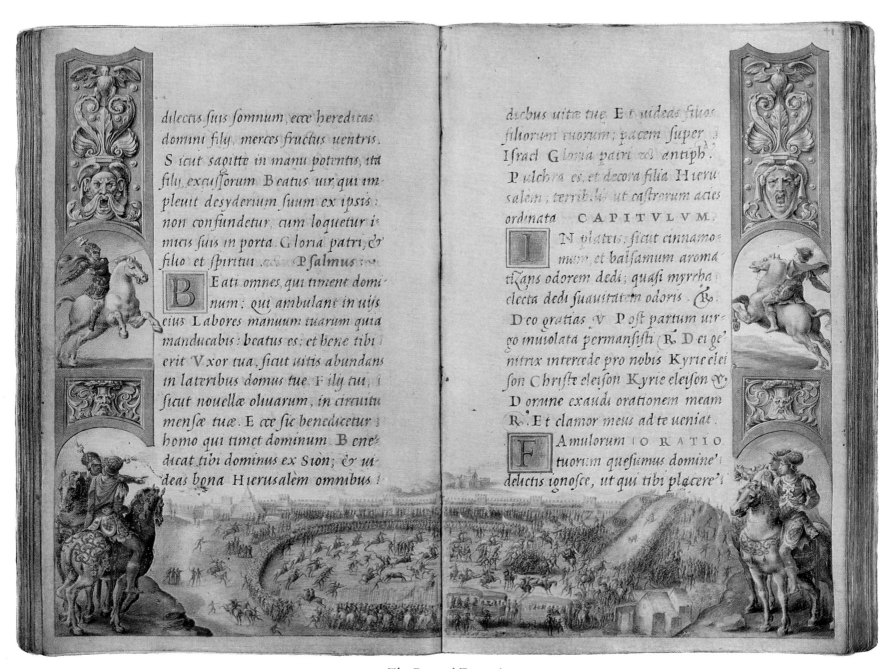

dilectis suis somnum, ecce hereditas
domini filij, merces fructus uentris.
Sicut sagitte in manu potentis, ita
filij excussorum Beatus uir, qui im-
pleuit desyderium suum ex ipsis:
non confundetur, cum loquetur i-
micis suis in porta. Gloria patri, &
filio et spiritui .... Psalmus

Beati omnes, qui timent dominum; qui ambulant in uijs
eius Labores manuum tuarum quia
manducabis; beatus es; et bene tibi
erit Uxor tua, sicut uitis abundans
in lateribus domus tue. Filij tui,
sicut nouellæ oluarum, in circuitu
mensæ tuæ. Ecce sic benedicetur
homo qui timet dominum Benedicat tibi dominus ex Sion; & uideas bona Hierusalem omnibus

diebus uitæ tuæ. Et uideas filios
filiorum tuorum; pacem super
Israel Gloria patri ... antiph.
Pulchra es, et decora filia Hierusalem; terribilis ut castrorum acies
ordinata CAPITVLVM.

IN plateis, sicut cinnamo-
mum, et balsamum aroma-
tizans odorem dedi; quasi myrrha
electa dedi suauitatem odoris. ...
Deo gratias. ... Post partum uir-
go inuiolata permansisti R. Dei ge-
nitrix interæde pro nobis Kyrie elei
son Christe eleison Kyrie eleison &.
Domine exaudi orationem meam
R. Et clamor meus ad te ueniat.

FAmulorum IORATIO.
tuorum quæsumus domine
delictis ignosce, ut qui tibi placere

The Feast of Testaccio,
fo. 40 v and 41, Farnese Book of Hours, New York, Pierpont Morgan
Library

The Flight Into Egypt,
fo. 42 v, Farnese Book of Hours, New York, Pierpont Morgan Library

The Crossing of the Red Sea,
fo. 43, Farnese Book of Hours, New York, Pierpont Morgan Library

Shortly after Franscisco dé Hollanda's visit, between 1539 and 1540, Clovio left Palazzo Grimani and entered into the service of Alessandro Farnese, who gave him a room in his own house, two servants and a horse, but often neglected to pay him.[56] Notwithstanding such an inconvenience, this was the happiest moment in Clovio's life. He had already become part of an artistic élite which included Michelangelo, Vignola, Antonio da Sangallo, Perin del Vaga, Salviati, Venusi, Daniele da Volterra, Parmigianino and Bertoia, Titian, El Greco, the Zuccaris, Pulzone, Vasari, Muziano and Spranghe. He saw in the prince's favor

the offical recognition of his merits and in his protection the promise of an assured celebrity. The *Gran Cardinale* was an influential patron whose "neofeudal" will practically dictated the artistic tendencies in Rome after 1540. He was responsible for the evolution of taste which resulted in the subjection of Renaissance ideals and thought to a "gothic revival". The fortune of the miniature improved in this climate; the medieval art was reborn. Beside Clovio, *il principe dei miniatori,* there was the Frenchman Raymond Vincent who, in 1549, was nominated the lifelong miniaturist of the Papal Chapel and Sacristy of Paul III,

51

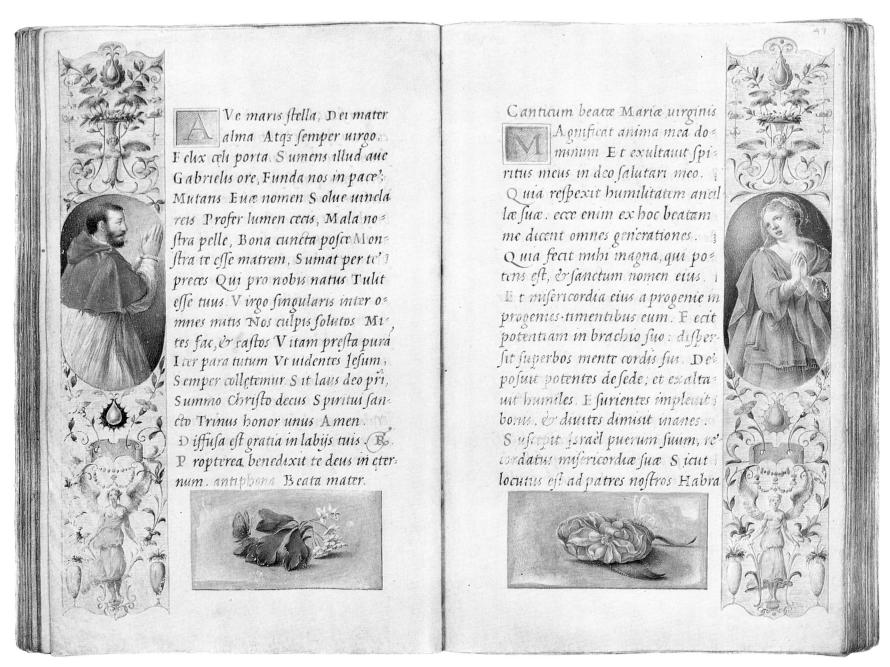

Cardinal Alessandro in Prayer, fo. 46 v and 47,
Farnese Book of Hours, New York, Pierpont Morgan Library

The Coronation of the Virgin,
fo. 48 v, Farnese Book of Hours, New York, Pierpont Morgan Library

Esther Crowned by Ahasuerus,
fo. 49, Farnese Book of Hours, New York, Pierpont Morgan Library

and Apollonio de'Bonfratelli da Capranica who also served the Pope from 1523 to 1572 as miniaturist of *capellae et sacrestiae apostolicae.* The former was author of the *Book of Psalms* (Paris, Bibliotheque Nationale, ms. 8880) that — in its homage to the Raphael and Michelangelo — was for some time thought to be Clovio's.[57] Apollonio de'Bonfratelli painted an *Obeisance of the Shepherds* (London, British Museum, ms. Add. 21412), also of an eminently Roman character. Vespasiano Strada, according to Baglione, was also a miniaturist. Of his work there remains a small parchment mounted on copper in the Galleria Pal-

lavicini, a copy of the *Crucifixion* by Taddeo Zuccari of 1556[58]. None of them can be compared to Clovio for ability and culture but, like him, they belonged in the well-defined climate which conditioned their inspiration according to the mystic requirements of the neomedieval wave.

For his new employer Clovio painted his masterpiece the *Officium Virginis,*[59] (Morgan Library, New York). The enthusiastic Vasari writes[60] it cost the proud illustrator nine years of work (nearly thirty years later he was portrayed by El Greco in the portrait of Capodimonte,

The Creation,
fo. 59 v, Farnese Book of Hours, New York, Pierpont Morgan Library

The Holy Family,
fo. 60, Farnese Book of Hours, New York, Pierpont Morgan Library

holding the little codex open in his right hand) and was completed in 1546. The Morgan codex is a compendium of Clovio's intelligent interpretation of the Roman, and Tuscan styles, a splendid summary of preceding trails as well as a display of a, by then, thirty-year culture. It is a confluence of memories, suggestions, and stimuli. Every accusation of "servile coping" falls before such an inexhaustible capacity for "manipulation" in the sense of inventive imagination. The raw materials are the Sistine frescoes, the Raphael Stanzas, and the Vatican Loggias, three generators of endless acrobatic experiments. The scope of Clovio's experience ranges from the pathos of the spreading noemedieval movement, to the pre-romantic evasiveness of ephemeral landscapes, to the over-elaborate caprices of the grotesque. This restless inventiveness is the sign of an intellect fleeing before a tremendous spiritual crisis. No longer the searcher, the quester in the abyss, the artist expresses himself in decorative forms. Rarely does a glimmer of anything deeper shine through.

The ecclesiastic patrons of this period were less liberal than their predecessors. They often dictated the dogmas and prejudices found in both the style and content of many

The Death of Uriah,
fo. 63 v, Farnese Book of Hours, New York, Pierpont Morgan Library

David in Prayer,
fo. 64, Farnese Book of Hours, New York, Pierpont Morgan Library

paintings; these are often so complex as to make one suspect the control of theological authorities at the artist's side. Clovio, in his masterwork, *The Officium Virginis,* raised a true monument to the academic and doctrinaire sensibility of Counter Reformation Rome. As a man of the court in every way he possessed neither the vital tension nor the daring originality of an artist who travels alone on the road reserved for free geniuses.

The men of the second generation of mannerism were bound to the first generation. In Clovio we find a grateful homage to the Michelangeloesque dictatorship in the *Bronze Serpent* (fo. 103), and to the manner of Raphael in the *Prophecy of the Birth of Christ to King Achaz* (fo. 5)[61] and in the *Meeting Between Solomon and the Queen of Sheba* (fo. 39) and the *Holy Family* (fo. 60). His education through Dürer is shown in the *Temptation* (fo. 27), his studies of antiquity in the *Grimani Evangelistary*[62], the *Tower of Babel* (fo. 107), and certain floral motifs of a naturalistic taste (fo. 46v—47). From the flexible Parmigiaminesque formulas are derived the linear models of the *Visitation* (fo. 17v) and *Justice and Peace Embracing* (fo. 18); these have become more fragile, ready to melt into

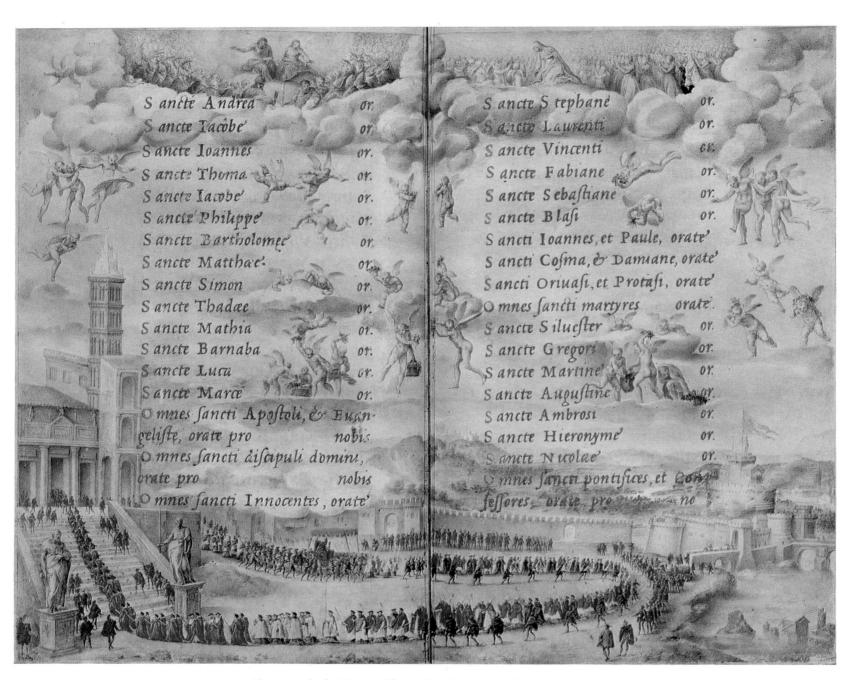

Sancte Andrea   or.
Sancte Iacobe   or.
Sancte Ioannes   or.
Sancte Thoma   or.
Sancte Iacobe   or.
Sancte Philippe   or.
Sancte Bartholomee   or.
Sancte Matthæe   or.
Sancte Simon   or.
Sancte Thadæe   or.
Sancte Mathia   or.
Sancte Barnaba   or.
Sancte Luca   or.
Sancte Marce   or.
Omnes sancti Apostoli, & Euan-
geliste, orate pro   nobis
Omnes sancti discipuli domini,
orate pro   nobis
Omnes sancti Innocentes, orate

Sancte Stephane   or.
Sancte Laurenti   or.
Sancte Vincenti   or.
Sancte Fabiane   or.
Sancte Sebastiane   or.
Sancte Blasi   or.
Sancti Ioannes, et Paule, orate
Sancti Cosma, & Damiane, orate
Sancti Oriuasi, et Protasi, orate
Omnes sancti martyres   orate.
Sancte Siluester   or.
Sancte Gregori   or.
Sancte Martine   or.
Sancte Augustine   or.
Sancte Ambrosi   or.
Sancte Hieronyme   or.
Sancte Nicolae   or.
Omnes sancti pontifices, et Con-
fessores, orate pro   no

Litany with the Corpus Christi Day Procession, fo. 72 v and 73,
Farnese Book of Hours, New York, Pierpont Morgan Library

The Resurrection of Lazarus,
fo. 80, Farnese Book of Hours, New York, Pierpont Morgan Library

The Triumph of Death,
fo. 79 v, Farnese Book of Hours, New York, Pierpont Morgan Library

Bertoia's docile creatures who seem to make a path for the foamy horses (fo. 43).

The Farnese *Officium* is rich in motifs and models, and served practically as a didactic institution for the younger artists who came to the Farnese Palace after 1546 and paid homage to the "prince of miniaturists" (we have already mentioned Sprangher). Consider the *Adoration of the Shepherds* (fo. 26)[63], the Raphaelesque and Sebastianesque theme of the Madona with the veil.

The Visitation, (fo. 17 v) is modeled after Battista Franco's *Nativity* (Sta. Maria Sopra Minerva, Rome) although in style it recalls Salviati, whose crowded surfaces and spaces without backgrounds in the paintings in S. Giovanni Decollato are recapitulated in the bold foreshortenings and complex compositions of the *Officium*. Clovio paid Salviati back for what he had borrowed: in the frames of the latter's frescoes in the Pallio Chapel and in the Ricci Palace, the rich decorative use of architectonic elements seems like

The Crucifixion,
fo. 102 v, Farnese Book of Hours, New York, Pierpont Morgan Library

The Bronze Serpent,
fo. 103, Farnese Book of Hours, New York, Pierpont Morgan Library

a large-scale translation of the work Clovio had carried out in miniature. Salviati has, through Clovio, almost returned to the *gran maniera* from which these motifs had originated.

Bronzino's golden and glacial vision, so far from the pungent, vivacious taste of Salviati, also made its mark on Clovio. We see it in the insertions of portraits (according to Vasari[64]) of the members of the Farnese court: the lovely Settimia and Mancina on fo. 34v, that of a dwarf on

fo. 39, those of Alessandro and Lucrezia Farnese on fo. 46v and 47, and that of Ottavio Farnese on fo. 49.

The urgency of their realism interrupts the decorative context of the Morgan pages. These characters are completely indifferent to the occasion which they are called upon to assist. They anticipate the taste with which Taddeo Zuccari, in the Caprarola, was to paint slight, nearly casual images notwithstanding the solemn and courteous destination of the work. The example of the compositions

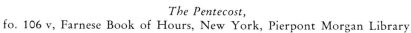

The Pentecost,
fo. 106 v, Farnese Book of Hours, New York, Pierpont Morgan Library

The Building of the Tower of Babel,
fo. 107, Farnese Book of Hours, New York, Pierpont Morgan Library

(fo. 80; fo. 102v) which, having overcome the rage of the pursuing culture, become slimmer and simpler in an antique proto-Raphaelesque composure, must certainly have influenced Marcello Venusti's and Siciolante da Sermoneta's mystic inclinations.

In spite of the attentive and sensitive exegeses of contemporary criticism,[65] the problem of Clovio's teaching in the formation of the young El Greco has not been faced yet. He was certainly a teacher as well as friend,[66] during

his stay in Rome. The Orsini inventory[67] lists small-sized works by El Greco from this period, and the *Portrait of a Man* of the Hispanic Society of America, New York, bears witness to his activity as a miniaturist. In the works done in Rome (that is, the *Expulsion from the Temple* of Minneapolis and the *Healing of the Blindman* of the Pinacoteca, Parma) the dense backgrounds with waving architecture on a diagonal perspective, the ample figures with disproportionately small heads, the coloring stimulated in unusual combinations refer closely to the lesson of the *Officium Virginis.*

Clovio's really great inventions are the margins, which the "horror vacui" drives him to overload with a superabundance of fashionable motifs. These point to the profoundly mannerist aspect of his creativity. The "Raphael venture" from Giulio Romano to Perin del Vaga, from Polidoro to Giovanni da Udine, was the bottomless coffer from which Clovio pulls out handfuls of giants, putti, light little temples and waving ribbons, bizarre masks and sensuous Venuses, trophies, caryatides, mysterious hooded figures, oriental knights and sphinxes, capitals, pearls, and flowers. Everything is massed and crowded into the space, so packed at times as to seem on the point of falling, unable to support so much pomp. As coordinating elements or supporting motifs to the borders and grotesques, Clovio frequently inserts landscapes which do not relate directly to the narrative except in precise circumstances such as *The Feast of Testaccio* (fo. 40v—41) or the *Corpus Dominus Procession* (fo. 72v—73) in which the rendering

of the architectonic annotations in the swarming "piles of ants" of a Vasarian stamp is absolutely faithful. Otherwise the scenes spread out for the addition of heterogeneous elements such as the Renaissance castles and temples, the ruins and obelisks, the villages, the mountains and seas. All coexist on an elastic plan of an extremely simple structure. The *Bay* of *Naples* (fo. 20v—21) the *Island of Tiberina* (fo. 50v—51) and the shores of *Sicily with Etna* (fo. 66v—67) are so devoid of realistic implications as to appear equally as fabulous as the invented landscapes,

transient pauses of blue and green. Perspectives are stolen from the geometrical rule and bent to the same decorative function as the margins. The example of Dossi's landscapes and the tidings from Fontainebleau, which in those same years was maturing joyfully in the fable of Niccolo dell' Abate, can only partly explain the delicate moors with flexible birds flying above. They may also represent Clovio's distillation of the Flemish experience. This certainly began before 1530 when, in the Grimani household, Clovio practiced on the works of the Northern masters besides

Dürer who formed such a large part of that collection: two portraits by Memling, three canvases by Patinir and three by Bosch, not to mention the famous *Breviary*[68].

During the following years of contact with the rich Farnese collection and their librarian Fulvio Orsini, Clovio saw more evidence of Flemish art. He even owned one or two examples. Above all the precise and minute representations by Joachim Patinir must have appealed to his miniaturist's perceptive subtlety. He would have admired the diluting of lines in the vaporous atmosphere, the barely tangible succeeding plains, the indented profiles of pale blue fortresses disappearing in the distance of a chromatic perspective that recalls Leonardo. "That which you want to be five times more distant make it five times more blue — *quello che voi che sia cinque volte piu lontano, fallo cinque volte piu azzurro*".

The death of the Pope Paul III Farnese and the election in February 1550, of Julius III, who was unfavorably disposed towards his predecessor's family, forced Cardinal Alessandro to leave Rome for Florence where Clovio fol-

lowed him. Still combining the small size *"da gabinetto"* and the technique of the miniature, he painted a parchment for Cosimo I de'Medici, the *Crucifixion with Mary Magdalen* and the *Pietà* now in the Uffizi.[69] The vicinity of the works of the Florentine mannerists, of Pontormo and Bronzino, explains the light that sharpens the outlines of both works and blocks the pathetic sentimentality of the characters in a dazzling firmness.

Clovio also assmilated the new sensibility of painters such as Venusti and Siciolante (working in Rome during those years) which expressed itself in a filtering and toning down of the Michelangelesque model (see Venusti's copy of Michelangelo's *Pietà* for Vittoria Colonna at the Borghese Gallery, Rome). Michelangelo's hegemony still prevailed in the new religious iconography in the works of Scipione Pulzone and Muziano. This reformed, or "counter-reformed" Michelangelism was accessible only to the faithful and often monotonous. Clovio descends to this kind of schematic representation in devout themes like the Crucifixion and the Pietà.[70]

The soft, detailed landscape of the Uffizi *Crucifixion* recalls Clovio's early predilection for the Flemish style. It may also be related to Clovio's meeting with Brueghel which took place in Rome in 1553. The proof of this meeting is not only to be found in the inventory of Clovio's possessions[71] but also in that very suggestive little miniature of a storm at sea (De Tolnay[72] would have it as being of Brueghel's hand) in the lower margin of the sheet (fo. 23v) which Clovio illuminated for the *Towneley Lectionary.* The dating of this work is still disputed.[73] With W. Smith[74],

I prefer the period between 1550 and 1560, proposed by De Tolnay, which finds confirmation in the collaboration between Clovio and Brueghel.

The Townley miniatures felt the effect of the spiritual crisis in Roman art of that decade. The artists' attempts to revitalize an exausted invented power often manifested itself in a sterile eclecticism. Still, there are moments of energy and power, notably in the *Resurrection* (fo. 16v), full of blazing contortions and whirlpools of light. Many of the same features can found in the work by Marco del

Pino on the same theme (*Resurrection,* Borghese Gallery, Rome, 1555 c.). In contrast to the mystical-metaphysical blaze of the *Resurrection,* the *Calling of the Apostles* (fo. 6v) shows a punctual intent narrative, giving attention to the physiognomical study of the lined-up figures, following the taste of the school headed by Zuccari. The same margins, even though composed of the usual elements, appear more sober than those of the Morgan codex.

One feels that the sobriety is a little due to weariness, certainly due to the bewilderment of an intellect tired of inventing and choosing. There is a discontinuous unbalanced *Nativity* (fo. 5v) where the single forms, in themselves resplendent with terse colors, do not add up to a harmonic whole (which the artist recovers in the emphatic *Last Judgement* (fo. 23v) resorting to the structures of his Michelangelesque and Raphaelesque repertory). Clovio, always a man of his time, wavers between the mystic languors of the art of the Counter Reformation and the celebrative intentions of the "neofeudal" court using — as his contemporaries did — a language which threatened to become a

repeatable form *ad infinitum.* The Towneley miniatures, if not the happiest from the point of view of invention and possibly execution, are nonetheless unique in their clear depiction of the restlessness of that epoch.

In 1556 Clovio was at Parma, the guest of Cardinal Alessandro Farnese's brother Ottavio (which forces us to place the painting of the *Towneley Lectionary* between 1553 and 1556, admitting of course that it was already completed before his departure); in 1557—1558 he was at Piacenza where he underwent an operation in his left eye;

in 1559 he went to Correggio and in 1560 he was at Candiana to renew his permission to live outside the monastery[75]. In 1565 he returned permanently to Rome. Mirella Levi D'Ancona[76] places three miniatures from the Wildenstein collection in this period: *Holy Family with an Armed Figure*, a *Holy Family with Saint Elizabeth*[77] and a *David and Goliath*[78]. Once again there is a contrast between the motionless monumental figures of the first two, to be placed in the ambit of the Florentine culture of Bronzino and Salviati (for the second one can also speak of a Parmi-

gianinesque influence), and the third, a sliding of crushing plains one upon the other to be placed in the years in Rome after 1560. In Florence and Emilia Clovio acquired the mystery of the ephebic warriors, of androgynous maidens, of dignified alabaster profiles, of eyes devoid of any passion. He gathered these characters around Madonnas of flourishing forms pressed in Salviatesque clothes in suffocating spaces, further strained by the oblique shapes of a stall and a step. Once in Rome Clovio keeps the pale cold colors of Tuscan mannerism while experimenting with new uses of light and the deformed geometry of perspectives moving on centrifugal axes. In *David and Goliath,* the light slides off the garments glued to the flesh, highlighting the restless asymmetry. Clovio may have used Daniele of Volterra's *David and Goliath* — now in the Louvre — as a prototype. Certainly he saw it in Florence, where it had

caused great commotion in the fifties. Clovio replaced Daniele's plastic violence and chiaroscuro reliefs by unstable foreshortenings and lights without contrasts. The same entwining of arms of the youth and the muscular giant loses harshness in Clovio's interpretation. The battle assumes an ambiguous grace, a Tasso-like sweetness more like an embrace than a deadly fight. Nothing remains of his work after 1560, though Vasari lists several works for the Duke Cosimo, the Marchesa of Pescara and for the Emperor Massimiliano[79] showing continual activity, though less intensive due to his advanced years. The infirmity of his eyes made work difficult; neither the waters of Lucca nor the treatment of a skillful doctor in Venice in July, 1560, proved beneficial. To these last years we can attribute two beautiful works conserved in the depository of the Sabauda Gallery in Turin. They have traditionally been attributed

74

IL VERISSIMO RITRATTO DEL SANTISSIMO SVDARIO
DEL NOSTRO SALVATORE GIESV CHRISTO

OREMVS.
DEVS QVI NOBIS IN SANCTA SINDONE, QVA CORPVS TVVM SACRATISSIMV
È CRVCE DEPOSITVM À IOSEPH INVOLVTVM FVIT, PASSIONIS TVÆ VESTIGIA
RELIQVISTI, CONCEDE PROPITIVS, VT PER MORTEM, ET SEPVLTVRAM TVAM AD
RESVRRECTIONIS GLORIAM PERDVGAMVR.QVI VIVIS, ET.C.

to Clovio, notwithstanding the lack of documentary evidence. One consists of four scenes of the *Passion*[80] and the other represents the *Holy Shroud*[81].

In the Passion the crystalline chromatic connections and volumes taken from various epochs and cultures are synthesized and scanned by a classical rule. The form of the *Deposition* belongs to the Raphaelesque tradition; that of the *Flagellation* alludes to Titian's example *Christ on the Mount of Olives,* and to the Venetian School of the *quattrocento.* Following simple outlines the landscapes open calmly, forgetful of past storms. Peaceful figures are set in place, without compression or contortion. If it were not for some arrangements and features distilled from the Northern schools, particularly in *The Flagellation* and in the *Crucifixion,* one could venture that Clovio had overcome the "Manner" and the new classicism. The *Holy*

Shroud shows an even more conventional compositive form. The regular and refined borders are laid out in the longobsolete design of the illuminated page. The dead Christ, the group of devout women, the angels in the sky, the facing ladders which disappear in a heavy bank of clouds, and the little landscape at the bottom behind the hill still follow the formula of the "regulated blending". Invention and experimentation have by now been clearly exhausted. There remains only the ability of a hand which has painted for at least fifty years and which knows the subtleties of lines and all the shades of colors from the most tender of pinks to the darkest of browns.

Clovio's spirituality lacked the mystical aspirations that burned in the sensibility of El Greco. The two Eastern artists both traveled to the West from ancient lands where the religious spirit had never rejected the imagination as

The Passion of Christ, Turin, Sabauda Gallery

Deposition, Milan, private collection

the evocator of images ardent with sensuality. In Rome they had both met a figurative culture which, though based upon Renaissance naturalism, was concerned with distorting forms. The had both bent these forms towards an embittered mold but, while the Cretan, in the solitude of Toledo, extolled the style to the point of making it only "the mirror . . . of his mystic and passionate soul" (Palluchini, 1937), the Croat, a prisoner of the suffocating atmosphere of the Eternal City, ended up being crushed by memories, prejudices and doctrine. Who knows if Clovio was aware

of the danger? At seventy[82] he was less anxious but sadder, still half way between the Court and the Church. He had not resolved the torment of ambivalences which were of his epoch, but he had renounced the search for a way out. "He waited for nothing other", Vasari wrote[83] "than to procure the health of his soul with good and holy works and with a life withdrawn from the things of the world."

Giulio Clovio died in the Farnese Palace on January 5th, 1578 and was buried in Rome in the church of San Pietro in Vincoli.

NOTES

1. G. VASARI, *Le Vite... La Vita di Giulio Clovio* (edited by G. Previtali, P. Ceschi, F. Negri Arnoldi), vol. VII, p. 439 and 446.

2. P. PINO, *Dialogo della pittura* in P. BAROCCHI, *Trattati d'Arte del Cinquecento*, Bari 1960—62, 1, p. 126.

3. R. BORGHINI, *Il Riposo... in cui della Pittura e della Scultura si Favella*, Florence 1584, p. 434—436 and 499.

4. G. P. LOMAZZO, *Trattato dell'Arte della Pittura Scultura ed Architettura* (1984), Rome 1844, vol. II, p. 382.

5. G. MANCINI, "Considerazioni sulla Pittura", in A. MARUCCHI, *Fonti e Documenti Inediti per la Storia dell'Arte*, I, p. 93, ed Academia Nazionale dei Lincei 1956.

6. G. BAGLIONE, *Vite de'Pittori, Scultori, Architetti del Pontificato di Gregorio XIII del 1572 fino a Quello di Urbano VIII del 1642*, Rome 1642 (edited bö V. Mariani, Rome 1935) p. 14—16.

7. L. LANZI, *Storia Pittorica d'Italia*, Bassano 1818, vol. IV, p. 18.

8. The painting, now in the Institute of Arts of Minneapolis (cat. no. 105), is to be dated between 1570 and 1575 for its identity of Clovio's face with that of the same person in the "Portrait" at Capodimonte (Naples) done by El Greco for Fulvio Orsini, the art-collecting librarian of the Farnese household.

9. F. BALDINUCCI, *Notizie dei Professori del Disegno da Cimabue in Qua*, Milan 1846—47, V, p. 106—116.

10. F. DE BONI, *Biografie degli Artisti*, Venice 1840, p. 231—232.

11. J. SAKCINSKI, *Život Juria Klovia slikara. Prinesak za Povèstnicu Umètnosti Slavenske.* Zagreb 1852—1858; and "Klovio" in *Lexicon of South Slovenic Artists* 1852.

12. J. W. BRADLEY, *Life and Works by Giulio Clovio*, London 1891.

13. A. M. BESSONE AURELI, *Introduzione Note e Bibliografia alla "Vita di Don Giulio Clovio Miniatore" di G. Vasari*, Florence Milan Pisa Naples 1915.

14. F. BONNARD, *Un Hôte du Palais Farnese: Don Giulio Clovio*, Paris 1929.

15. A. BACOTICH, Giorgio Giulio Clovio, 1498—1578 *(Dalmata?)*, in Archivio Storico per la Dalmazia, XI, vol. XX, 1936, p. 422—46.

16. J. A. HEBERT, *Clovio*, in "Thieme Becker, Allgemeines Lexikon der Bildenden Künstler", VII 1912, p. 122—124.

17. A. E. BYE, Two Clovio Manuscripts in New York, in *Art in America*, V, February 1917, p. 88—89.

18. M. LEVI D'ANCONA; "Illuminations by Clovio Lost and Found" in *Gazette des Beaux Arts*, 1950, p. 55—76.

19. W. SMITH, "Giulio Clovio and the Maniera di Figure Piccole", in *Art Bulletin*, 1964, p. 395—401.

20. For historical documentation concerning the artist's life see A. RONCHINI, G. Clovio in *Atti e Memorie della R. Deputazione di Storia patria per le province Modenese e Parmese* 1865, III, p. 259—270; M. ABERTOLOTTI, "Don Guilio Clovio Principe dei Miniatori", in "*Atti e Memorie delle Deputazioni di Storia Patria per l'Emilia e la Romagna*", N. S. VII, p. 11 Modena 1882, p. 267—272 and Don Giulio Clovio Principe dei Miniatori in "*Il Bibliofilo*", III, 1882, p. 88—89.

21. According to Sakcinski (op. cit., note 12), while in the whole Croatian coast there is no document which records the name Clovio, there are frequent surnames such as Glovičić and Glavičić in Grižane and in Novi Glovan and Glavon in Trsat, Globić again in Grižane, Glavić in Bosnia and then in Dalmatia and along all the Croatian coast. It is possible that Clovio's family, like many others, came from Macedonia, and had emigrated in the retinue of the Uscochi into Croatia. This would explain why Clovio, besides "Crovatinus", "Crovata", "Illiricus", "di Crovatia" and "de Croatia", at times also signed himself "Macedonus". Bacotich (op. cit., note 16) on the other hand refers to the existence of names such as Clovio, Clodio and de Clavis in Dalmatia and in the Morlacca provinces and he is anxious — in 1936! — to maintain them as "Dalmaticita".

22. Not by Marino Grimani, who only became Cardinal in 1526, after the death of his uncle Domenico in 1523 (cf. P. PASCHINI, *Domenico Grimani Cardinal di S. Marco* (+ 1523, Rome 1943). We do not know how Clovio got to know this influential person. He could have been recommended to him by a member of the family of the Frankopan Counts who, at one time, were lords of the district of Vinodol, which included the village of Grižane; or, when still in his homeland, he could have personally met Domenico Grimani, whose father Admiral Antonio,

the commander-in-chief of the Venetian Army, had been exiled (following the defeat suffered from the Turks in 1498) to the islands of Cres and Osor.

23. For the importance of the Grimani family with regard to maneristic culture see also J. SCHULZ, *Venetian Painted Ceilings of the Renaissance*, University of California 1968.

24. G. VASARI, op. cit., VII, p. 440.

25. Nothing remains of the young miniaturist's activities in Hungary, unless one wishes to recognize his hand in the precious *Missal* (MR 354) written at the end of the XV cent. for Canon Juraj de Topusko, preserved in the Cathedral Treasury in Zagreb. D. KNIEWALD *(Misal Čazmanskog Prepošta Jurja de Topusko i Zagrebačkog biskupa Šimuna Erdödy,* Zagreb 1944, p. 66—79; *Iluminacija i Notacija Zagrebačkih Liturgijskih rukopisa,* Zagreb 1944, p. 79—81) distinguishes two styles in the miniature which decoraters the *Missal* (MR 354), "gothic in the first part it is to be considered in connection with miniature art current in Hungary during the last thirty years of the XV cent., the second part is Italian Renaissance in conformity with the style at the court of Buda during the first thirty years of the XVI cent. (that is in sheets 17, 27, XVIII', LXIII', CV', CXXXII', CLIII', CLIV', CLXX', CC', CCIX', CCXIII', CCXXXIX', CCXXXIX')". For the first group of miniatures D. Kniewald names Johanes Hans pictor Almanus, for the second, taking up an old supposition of Sakcinski's (I. SAKCINSKI KUKULJEVIĆ *Prvostolna Crkva Zagrebačka,* Zagreb 1856, p. 58—59; *Julio Klovio,* Zagreb 1878, p. 66), he names Giulio Clovio. The elements in favour of this second identification are above all to be found in the chronology: the pages of the *Missal* (MR 354), in which Kniewald recognizes the "Italian Renaissance" style, all carry the coat-of-arms of the Bakač-Erdödy family, a stag on a half wheel, surmounted by a bishop's hat; as Šimun Erdödy was the Bishop of Zagreb from 1518 to 1543 the decoration of the second group of pages of the *Missal* (MR 354) must be held within these limits. Besides, bearing in mind the fact that the illustrations of the Zagreb codex are incomplete, Kniewald tightens the chronological extremes indicating 1526, the year of the Mohač catastrophe, when because of the lack of money and of artists it would have been impossible to terminate the work, the "terminus post quem non" of the carrying out of the miniature, so making the years 1518—1526 coincide with those of the young Clovio's stay in Buda (1524—1526). The second argument in favour of Clovio's collaboration in the decoration of the *Missal* (MR 354) is a monogram, included among the arabesques of the slim candelabrum which divides the text of fo. CXXXII' into two parts, in fact one of those pages with Bishop Erdödy's coat-of-arms. It is a small red shield, leaning against a crossed sceptre and sword, on which some mysterious gilded letters are interwoven to form a monogram, which according to Kniewald (op. cit. 1940, p. 68) should be read as "Julio Clovio", the signature therefore of the miniaturist of those pages. To the objection that the Croatian artist only took the name of "Giulio" after 1527, one can answer that Vasari (ed. 1965, VII, p. 439) wrote "... *and his baptismal name was Juraj Julije*", suggesting that already beforehand, even though not officially, he used his second name. To which one can add the fact that the sumptuous borders of putti and foliage belong to the taste and manner of the Italian Renaissance, that certain Northern stylizations that can be retraced in the vignettes and in the typology are to be explained by his youthful exercises from Dürer, that the beautiful landscapes in the medallions, included in the margins of the Zagreb codex, seem to anticipate those characteristic of Clovio's mature period.
Another interesting suggestion for the *Missal* (MR 354) is the more recent one by I. BERKOVITZ *(Illuminated Manuscripts in Hungary,* Centuries XI—XVI, 1969, p. 92) who distinguishes three different hands in the pages of Šimun Erdödy's time, attributing only the landscapes of the medallions within the margins (sheets 17, VC', CXXXII', CLIII', CLXVI', CLXX', CC', CCIX', CCXIII', CCXXXIX', CCXLV') to Clovio.
In reality these landscapes form the most enchanting detail of the decoration of the Zagreb *Missal* (MR 354). A sharp, but very sensitive hand has traced the scenes of hunt, animals, woods, meandering rivers that are lost in the blue distances, the cities on the bare mountainous spurs and the country villages with pointed roofs; spell-bound by the delicate drawing and the domination of blue, we are tempted to recognize here an early announcement of the landscapes of the *Grimani Evangelistary* (Venice, Marciana Library, Lat. 1, 103). Dragutin Kniewald's and Ilona Berkovitz's hypotheses are extremely attractive, if confirmed they would fill the void that exists regarding Clovio's beginning. We have no work that can be placed in the years from his arrival in Italy, in 1516, to his flight from Rome, in 1527. All the same, at this point of studies and research, and on the basis of possible stylistic comparisons and documentary data, it is difficult for us to include, without perplexity, the *Missal* (MR 354) in the catalogue of Clovio's works.

26. G. VASARI, op. cit., VII, p. 441.

27. G. VASARI, op. cit., VII, p. 440.

28. For the miniatures *da gabinetto* see T. H. COLDING, *Aspects of Miniature Painting — Its Origins and Development,* Chap. IV, Copenhagen 1953.

29. This miniature has for a long time been "coupled" with another, of the same shape and of slightly inferior dimensions, showing the Marchioness of Dorset, with which it seems to be stylistically in accordance. From here a series of suppositions arise, from that of A. PRIMISSIER (in *MS Inventory of the Ambras Collection,* 1788, II, p. 275, no. 51), who believes the miniatures to be portraits of a married couple, to E. VON SACHEN (in *Die K. K. Ambrasen Sammlungen,* Vienna 1855, II, p. 113, no. 7 and 8) who, insisting on this idea, considers them both to be of the School of Holbein. G. F. WAAGEN (in *Die Vornstdentmaler in Wien,* Vienna 1866, II, p. 343) thinks the woman's portrait is later and by a different hand; and then J. SCHLOSSER in *Two portrait Miniatures from Castle Ambras,* in "Burlington Magazine", 1922 October, p. 194) maintains the man's portrait to be Clovio's self portrait and the woman's of the School of Holbein the Younger, explaining the traditional connection by their having probably belonged to Clovio's private collection. T. H. COLDING (op. cit., note 29, p. 78, fig. 54) without any doubt holds the man's portrait to be the Croatian miniaturist's "self-portrait".

30. G. VASARI, op. cit., VII, p. 450: "For I know of some private persons who have beautiful little portraits by him (Clovio), in small cases, of Lords, friends and women they love."

31. G. VASARI, op. cit., VII, p. 441: "*At that time (1530 circa) he did a great choir book with fine miniatures and lovely embellishments*". Compare also *MS Catalogue of Paintings Italian School ... of Consul Smith,* in "Burlington Magazine", XXIII, p. 161; A. E. POPHAM-J. WILDE, *The Italian Drawings of* XV *and XVI Centuries ... at Windsor Castle,* London 1949, no. 43, fig. 16; F. VIVIAN, *Il Console Smith Mercante e Collezionista,* Vicenza 1971, p. 84 and 195 (App. A. N. 345).

32. G. MARIANI CANOVA, *La Miniatura Veneta del Rinascimento,* Venice 1969.

33. G. VASARI, *Le Vite ... Vita di Gerolamo dei Libri,* Milan 1965 (edited by G. Previtali, P. Ceschi, F. Negri Arnoldi) V, p. 117: "*Gerolamo painted miniatures at Candiana ... and being here Giulio Clovio, a monk, learnt the principles of the miniature, he, who was to become the greatest in this art ...*" and at page 120 "*... Don Giulio Clovio, who had learnt it* (the art of the miniature) *from Gerolamo when he worked in Candiana ...*"

34. cf. *Italian Drawings Raphael and his Circle, Catalogue of Drawings of the British Museum,* no 95, no. 108, no. 163.

35. Venice, Biblioteca Marciana, Lat. I, 103. It was bought in 1932 by the Ministry of Education at the auction of the Chester Beatty Collection. Compare the *Catalogue of Renowned Western ms. of Chester Beatty,* London 1932, pages 58—59; *Catalogo della Mostra delle Biblioteche Italiane,* 1934; p. 31, no. 100.

36. M. LEVI D'ANCONA (op. cit., note 19) believes the *Evangelistary* at the Marciana to be Clovio's, while it is excluded by G. MUZZIOLI, *Mostra Storica Nazionale della Miniatura,* Florence 1953, no. 639.

37. The inventory of Clovio's possessions (cf. M. A. BERTOLOTTI op. cit. note 21, p. 15) includes also "a book of drawings and prints by Alberto".

38. Salviati came to Venice in '30, perhaps introduced to the Grimani by Clovio; later, in 1548, because of the Croatian miniaturist's good name, he obtained the commission for the frescoes of the Pallio Chapel at the Farnese Palace. cf. G. VASARI, *Le Vite ... La Vita di Francesco Salviati,* Milan 1965. (edited by G. Previtali, P. Ceschi, F. Negri Arnoldi), VI, p. 534.

39. J. W. BRADELY (op. cit., note 13), p. 67 and 367.

40. J. CHENEY, Francesco Salviati's North Italy Journey, in "*Art Bulletin*" 1963, p. 338, no. 7.

41. M. LEVI D'ANCONA, "Un Libro Scritto e Miniato da Giulio Clovio" in "*Contributi alla Storia del Libro Italiano*", Biblioteca di Bibliografia Italiana LXII, Miscellanea in Onore di Lamberto Donati", Florence 1969, p. 197—209.

42. Sheet 2 bears the inscription "*Fu cominciato questo libro P. dal Pre Julio Clovio Can. co. Reg. re*" in the margin.

43. The *Book of Hours* (Ms. 20927) was bought from Lord Stuart de Rothesay by the British Museum in 1835, where it is still to be found today. According to Vasari (op. cit., note 1, VII, p. 560) it was illuminated in Perugia; "an Office of Our Lady with four beautiful stories" cf. also *Societa Francese di Riproduzione dei Manoscritti*, 1914—20, II, p. 120; *British Museum — Reproductions from Illuminated Manuscripts*, IV, London 1928, p. 17—18; J. WARTROP, *Some aspects of Humanist Script (1460—1560)*, Oxford 1963, p. 32; M. LEVI D'ANCONA, op. cit., note 19.

44. The *Commentary to the Epistle of Saint Paul* (MS. II, London, Soane Museum) was most likely taken to England by Joseph Smith, the British Consul in Venice from 1740 to 1760. In 1801 it is listed in John Stange's *Catalogue* at Sotheby; it then belonged to Frederick Webbe and to the Duke of Buckingham; and in 1833 it was bought by Sir John Soane. Cf. E. G. MILIAR, Les Manuscrits a Peintures des Bibliothèques de Londres. Les Manuscripts à Peintures de la Bibliothèques du Musee de Sir John Soane, Lincoln's Inn Fields, Londres, in *"Bullettin de la Société Francaise de Reproductions de Manuscrits à Peintures"*, IV, no. 2, Paris 1914—1920, p. 116—126; G. F. WAAGEN, Über ein Manuscript mit Miniaturen des Don Giulio Clovio in *"Deutsches Kunstblatt"*, VII, 1850.

45. J. A. HERBERT, op. cit., note 17, p. 124.

46. The little medallion corresponds exactly to a lovely drawing in grey chalk in the library at Windsor. Cf. A. E. POPHAM-J. WILDE, op. cit., note 32, cat. no 243.

47. G. BAGLIONE, op. cit., note 6, p. 16: "Among some of his drawings reproduced in copper the fall of Saul in various attitudes of fear is famous...". In the Gabinetto delle Stampe of the Uffizi, Florence, there are two engravings (no. 1452 and 1453) identical to the British Museum drawing. On the back of one is the signature of "Dominus Vitus Vallis", it is dated 1577, and the other is a large indistinct drawing (324/Cor. V/T. 23), but certainly by Clovio. All the same the best known engraving of the "Conversion of Saint Paul" is the one by Cornelis Cort, 1576, done for Lorenzo Vaccaro (Bibl. Nat. Paris; Cabinet des Estampes, Ec.

48. Milan, Biblioteca Ambrosiana, Nicola da Bologna Room, no. 17. Cf. A. RATTI, *Guida Sommaria per il Visitatore della Biblioteca Ambrosiana e delle Collezioni Annesse*, Milan 1907, p. 52; E. TEA, *La Pinacoteca Ambrosiana di Milano*, 1932, p. 16; G. GALBIATI, *Itinerario per il Visitatore della Pinacoteca e dei Monumenti Annessi*, Biblioteca Ambrosiana, Milan 1951.

49. F. ZERI, *Pittura e Controriforma. Alle Origini dell'Arte Senza Tempo*, Turin 1957, p. 45.

50. The *Stanzes on the Venture of Aquila by Eurialo d'Ascoli* (MS. 2660, Vienna, Albertina Library) written by Monterchi are neither signed nor documented, but are traditionally attributed to Clovio on the basis of their unquestionable stylistic affinity to his certain works. Cf. *Società Francese di Riproduzione dei Manoscritti*, 1933, I, p. 42; H. J. HERMANN, *Die Handschriften und Incunabolen der Italianischen Renaissance. Mittelitalien: Toskane, Umbrien, Rome*, Leipzig 1932, p. 176—182, tav. LV—LVI. M. G. LA COSTE-MESSELIERE "Don Giulio" in *"L'Oeil"*, 1959, no. 52.

51. A. RONCHINI, op. cit., note 21.

52. F. DE HOLLANDA, *Dialoghi Michelangioleschi (Dialogo IV)* Rome 1926, p. 128. For "Ganymede" also see G. VASARI, op. cit. note 1, VII, p. 448; and M. A. BERTOLOTTI, op. cit., note 21, p. 14 line 11 and p. 12 line 17.

53. A. E. POPHAM-J. WILDE, op. cit., note 32, no. 457 and no. 459.

54. Bertolotti's inventory (op. cit., note 21) also lists "M. Michelangelo's dream done by the above mentioned Don Giulio"; "M. Michelangelo's *Phaeton* done by Don Giulio"; "A sheet of Michelangelo's putti (the *Bacchanal)* done by Don Giulio" and *"Tityus"*.

55. F. DE HOLLANDA, op. cit., note 53, p. 129, speaks of two large pages illuminated by Clovio, which correspond to the page with *"Saint Paul Blinding Elima"* (R. F. 3977, Paris, Louvre, Cabinet of Drawings and that of the "Three Theological Virtues" (R. F. 3978; Paris, Louvre, Cabinet of Drawings). In the same passage the Portuguese observes that in both of the miniatures: "Observing Don Giulio's miniatures I also noticed a special technique in the painting, based on certain dots which I call atoms, and in the guise of a fine veil of fabric seem like a mist fallen over the painting".
Cf. T. H. COLDING, op. cit., note 28, p. 68, fig. 103 and 104; M. G. DACOSTE-MESSELIERE, op. cit., note 51.

56. F. BONNARD, op. cit., note 15, p. 26—28.

57. J. SAKCINSKI, op. cit., note 12, p. 17; J. W. BRADLEY, op. cit., note 13, p. 262—270; L. DOREZ, *Le Psautier de Paul III*, Paris 1909.

58. F. ZERI, op. cit., note 50, p. 52.

59. The *Officium Virginis* (MS. 69, New York, Pierpont Morgan Library), in *ottava rima*, has on the last page a medallion inscribed "Julius Clovius, Macedo Monumenta Haec Alexandro Farnesio Cardinali Suo Domino faciebat MDXLV". The Cardinal died in 1589 and left the manuscript to his nephew Odoardo. Through a series of legacies, all withinthe ambit of the complicated Farnese family, the manuscript ended up in Naples in the Royal Library or Borbon Museum at the time of Francesco II, the last king of Naples. It became the property of his son Alfonso Di Borbone, whose mother, Maria Teresa of Austria, sent it to the Viennese court and entrusted it to the Archduke Ranieri. Through the mediation of the latter the manuscript was bought by Mr. P. Pierpont Morgan in 1903. It is bound in silver with an exquisite cover, the work of Antonio Gentili called Faenza.
Cf. A. E. BYE, op. cit., note 18; M. HAARSEN-G. K. BOYCE, *Italian Manuscripts in the Pierpont Morgan Library*, New York 1953, no. 102, W. SMITH, op. cit., note 20. There also exists a study by W. SMITH, *Master's Thesis of the Institute of Fine Arts*, New York University 1955.

60. G. VASARI, op. cit., note 1, VII, p. 445.

61. Another edition of the *"Christ's Prophecy to Achaz"* (fo. 5) and the *"Visitation"* (fo. 17 v) exists in Art Gallery of Auckland (New Zealand). They were probably preparatory drawings for the two scenes in the Morgan codex, but it is impossible to say so with certainty from the poor photographs in my possession.

62. In 1528 the *Grimani Evangelistary* (Venice, Marciana Library) belonged to the family of Clovio's first patrons.

63. Two lovely preparatory drawings of the *"Nativity"* (fo. 26) and of the *"Adoration of the Kings"* (fo. 38v) exist in the Royal Library, Windsor Castle. Cf. A. E. POPHAM-J. WILDE, op. cit., note 32, no. 241 and no. 245.

64. G. VASARI, op. cit., note 1, VII, p. 444.

65. R. PALLUCCHINI, "Il polittico del Greco alla R. Galleria Estense e la Formazione dell'Artista" in *"R. Istituto d'Archeologia e Storia dell'Arte-Opere d'Arte"*, VII, Rome 1937.

66. The continuity of a friendly relationship between the two artists was believed to be shown, not only in the letter of introduction to the Farnese family (cf., note no. 8), but also by another very suggestive letter in which Clovio tells of a visit he made to El Greco in his Roman atelier. Unfortunately HUGO KERHER, who published this document "Ein Besuch des Giulio Clovio in atelier Greco" in *"Kunstchronich und Kunstmarkt"*, 1922, N. F. 23, vol. 34°, p. (84—785) was deceived by a Croatian student, Jarko Fabrović, who in 1923 had given him to believe that he had found Clovio's original diary in the Civic Library of Split and had offered him a translation of the passage which told of the meeting between the two artists. I wish to thank Grgo Gamulin for this information and for indicating the magazine (*"Nedjeljna Dalmacija"*, 28 January 1973, p. 18), in which the extraordinary deception was unmasked.

67. P. DE NOLHAC, "Une Galerie de Peinture du XVI Siècle: les Collections de Fulvio Orsini" in *"Gazette des Beaux Arts"*, 1884, p. 433.

68. P. PASCHINI, op. cit., note no. 23, p. 160.

69. The two parchments (no. 241 and no. 812, Florence, Galleria degli Uffizi) have been cut out and stuck on to wood. The *"Pieta"* is signed "Iulius Clovius macodo faciebat" and the *"Crucifixion"* carries "Iulius Macedo f. 1553". Cf. M. LEVI D'ANCONA, op. cit., note 19; G. MUZZIOLI, op. cit., note 37, p. 496.

70. With regard to the composition of the *"Crucifixion"* one can refer to the illuminated page on canvas and the beautiful charcoal drawing in the British Museum (no 1895-9-15-1407 and no. 1860-16-16-19), and to that the pencil drawing (no 223173) of the Art Institute, Chicago, and the one in the British Museum (no. 1895-9-15-654). As for as the *"Deposition"* on parchment, in Museum of Duca di Martina, Naples, signed "J. Clovio R. fecit" (cf. I. A. MARESCA, vol. III, fasc. VI, April 1893; A. BACOTICH, op. cit., note 16) is concerned it can in no way be considered to be by Clovio because of its evident transcription from Federico Barocci's *"Deposition"* painted in 1582 for the Church of Santa Croce of Senigallia. The apocryphal signature is later and must

be accounted for by the fact that such was Clovio's celebrity that everything which had the flavour of the *cinquecento* miniature tended to be attributed to him. This also explains the otherwise incomprehensible "R" which appears nowhere else in Clovio's signature.

71. On page 11 of the inventory published by BERTOLOTTI (cf. op. cit., note 21) he mentions "A small miniature half done by himself Clovio and half by M. Pietro Brugole", "A gouache painting of Leon of France by the hand of M.ro Pietro Brugole" and on page 18 "Another village by Pietro Brugal" and "Another painting or village by Pietro Brugal".

72. CH. DE TOLNAY, Newly Discovered Miniatures by Peter Brueghel the Elder in the *"Burlington Magazine"* 1965, p. 110—114.

73. The *Towneley Lectionary* (M. 91, New York, Public Library) corresponds to the *Evangelistary* B. I. 12 given by Cardinal Farnese to the Sacristy of the Sistine Chapel, from where it was stolen by Napoleon's troops. Found and bought by John Towneley, it was donated to the Public Library. There are four full-page miniatures which are attributed to Clovio. Critics do not agree upon the date Cf. J. W. BRADLEY (op. cit., note 13, p. 351); A. E. BYE (op. cit., note 18, p. 88/99; M. LEVI D'ANCONA (op. cit., note 19, p. 55/74).

74. W. SMITH, op. cit., note 60, 1955.

75. A. RONCHINI, "G. Clovio", in *Atti e Memorie della R. Deputazione di Storia Patria per le Province Modenese e Parmese,* Modena, 1866, note 21. Ronchini published some letters of Clovio's addressed to Cardinal Farnese: from Piacenza 1/14/58/, from Correggio 7/9/60/ and 6/13/60, in which he complains of his illness and begs for help in his journey to Candiana.

76. M. LEVI D'ANCONA, op. cit., note 19, p. 70—74.

77. The miniature with the "Holy Family, Saint Elisabeth, Saint Joseph and three other figures" could be the one sent to Philip II's favorite Ruy Gomez de Silva, which is mentioned in a letter from Giuliano Ardinghelli, the Duke of Parma's ambasador in Brussels, addressed to Cardinal Farnese and dated 4th December 1556 (cf. A. RONCHINI, op. cit., note 21, p. 262) and stolen with three other miniatures from El Escorial in 1808. Cf. J. ZARCO CUEVAS, "Inventario de los Albrajos, Selicarios, Estatuas, Pinturas, Tapices y Objectos de Valor Curiosidad Donados por el Rey Felipe II al Monasterio El Escorial-Años 1571/1958" in *"Boletin de la Real Academia de la Historia",* vol. XCVII, Dec. 1930, p. 96.

78. According to a letter written by Annibal Caro, on behalf of Clovio to Margherita Farnese and dated 11th September 1561 (cf. E. MUENTZ,

"Une Lettre de Don Giulio Clovio à la Duchesse de Parma" in *"Archives des Arts",* 1, 1890, p. 71/72, another miniature, "Judith Putting the Head of Holofernes in a Bag", had been commissioned with that of "David and Goliath". To the former one can refer a charcoal drawing signed "Go. Julio Clovio" in the Gernsheim Collection, London (cf. the note in *"Burlington Magazine",* March 1937, p. 137) and an engraving by Soye (cf. J. C. J. BIERENS DE HAAN, L'Oeuvre Gravé de Cornelis Cort Graveur Hollandais 1533—1578, The Hague 1948, p. 42.

79. A print signed by Cornelis Cort in 1568 and 1569 carrying the inscription "Cum privilegio su pont. Don Iulius Clovius inv." (no. 1431) and two prints without any inscription (no. 1432 and no. 1433) in the Gabinetto delle Stampe e dei Disegni of the Uffizi, Florence, could be taken from the miniature destined for the emperor (cf. G. VASARI, op. cit., note 1, VII, p. 448 "Saint George killing the serpent in a beautiful village, worked with extreme care"). Another engraving again signed by Cort, but dated 1578, is preserved in the Gabinetto delle Stampe of the Vatican Library. Cf. J. C. J. BIERENS DE HAAN, op. cit., note 79, p. 138, no. 130. The edition of the same subject transcribed by Enea Vico (Bartsh, XV, 386, 12) in 1542 which carries the inscription "Julius Corvatin inv." is a different composition; therefore Clovio painted the same subject at least twice and at a distance of twenty years.

80. The "Passion" (cat. no. 150) of the Sabauda Gallery Turin, is formed with four miniatures on parchment placed in a contemporary frame so as to form an oval which was obviously supposed to hold another scene. Previously belonging to Cardinal Falconieri of Ravenna, it was sold by Baron Tecco to the gallery in 1574. Cf. G. PACCHIONI, *La Regia Pinacoteca di Torino,* Rome 1932, p. 14, no. 150; G. MUZZIOLI, op. cit., note 36, p. 495, no. 58; N. GABRIELLI, *Galleria Sabauda-Maestri Italiani,* Turin 1971, p. 108, no. 150, fig. 195.

81. The "Holy Shroud" (cat. no. 149) of the Sabauda Gallery Turin, is painted in water-colour on silk. Vittorio Emanuele II, to whom it seems to have been given by a noble from Cremona, gave it to the Pinacoteca in 1868. Cf. G. PACCHIONI, op. cit., note 81, p. 14, no. 149; M. G. LA COSTE MESSELIERE, op. cit., note 51; N. GABRIELLI, op. cit., note 81, p. 108, no. 149, fig. 194.

82. The "self-portrait" of the Uffizi Gallery, Florence — a small tondo painted on copper — is encircled with the inscription "D. Giulio Clovio miniatore" and in the background to the left there is a youthful profile. There is a "Portrait of Don Giulio" mentioned in the inventory of Clovio's possessions (cf. M. A. BERTOLOTTI, op. cit., note 21, p. 18, which could be this one. MUZZIOLI (op. cit.) note 37, p. 496, no. 60) dubitatively attributes it to the hand of the Croatian.

83. G. VASARI, op cit., note 1, VII, p. 450.

Madonna and Child,
detail fo. 14 r, Stuart de Rothesay Book of Hours,
London, British Museum

EL GRECO: *Portrait of Giulio Clovio,*
Naples, Museum of Capodimonte

CHICAGO, Art Institute, C. H. Gellosi, L. H. Gurley Coll (no. 223173)
Deposition

black pencil on paper (10 1/2 × 9 in). For the technique, the style and the strongly Michelangelesque characters, the drawing is to be associated with the signed *Deposition* of the British Museum (no. 1895-9-15-654) and that of Uffizi Gallery (no. 2457 F), and is therefore datable after 1540, in Clovio's mature period.

Bibliography

U. MIDDELDORF, 1939, p. 13-14; M. CIONINI-VISANI, 1971, p. 143, note 70, fig. 160.

FLORENCE, Uffizi
Self-portrait
tondo in oil on copper (diameter 4 5/8 in.)
The inscription *"D. Clovio/miniatore"* encircles it.

Perhaps it is the small portrait of Clovio listed by Sakcinski and Bradley and dubitatively attributed to Clovio by Muzzioli. The miniature, which reveals very fine workmanship, shows the artist in his later years, with the same features that one knows from the *Portrait* by El Greco (Capodimonte, Naples). In the dark background, behind his shoulders, there emerges a youthful profile. Considering the age of the model the little portrait is datable tetween 1565 and 1570. There are many witnesses to Clovio's activity as a portrait paiter (Vasari, De Nolhac). *"The Portrait of Don Giulio"* is remembered in the list of Clovio's possessions drawn up on January 4ht, 1578, and published bö Bertolotti, it could be this one. Besides, there are many portrait-like inserts in the decoration of the codices (ef. Soane Codex, Morgan Codex.)

Bibliography

M. A. BERTOLOTTI, 1882, p. 18; I. SAKCINSKI, 1882, p. 59; DE NOLHAC, 1884, p. 433; J. W. BRADLEY, 1891 and 1971, p. 352; G. MUZZIOLI, 1953, p. 496; M. CIONINI-VISANI, 1971, p. 114, note 82.

Deposition,
Chicago, Art Institute, C. H. Galosi, L. H. Gurley Collection

FLORENCE, Uffizi (no. 812)
Crucifixion with Mary Magdalen
tempera on parchment glued onto wood (9 1/2 × 6 3/4 in.)

Signed *"Iulius Macedo f. 1553"* at the bottom right, the miniature was recognized by Sakcinski as being the one done in Florence, 1553, for Cosimo I de'Medici and remembered by Vasari: *"For the said Lord Duke, Don Giulio did a Christ Crucified with the Magdalen at the foot of the Cross, which is such a wonderful ..."*. The miniature is close to a beautiful drawing (no. 1860-6-12-19) and an illuminated engraving (no. 1895-9-15-1407) of the British Museum, London, transcribed from Clovio's original by Cornelis Cort. The moving and soft body of the Crucified repeats the usual form of the mature Michelangelo. The Flemish landscape is immersed in a clear blue light and shows a fantasttic view of Jerusalem. Among the buildings the round construction of the Holy Grave is recognizable.

Bibliography

G. VASARI, 1550 and 1568, ed. 1965, VII, p. 447; I. SAKCINSKI, 1852, p. 25; J. W. BRADLEY, 1891 and 1971, p. 353; M. Levi D'ANCONA, 1950, p. 66, p. 70; G. MUZZIOLI, 1953, p. 496; M. CIONINI-VISANI, 1971, p. 136.

An Armed Mounted Soldier Slaying Two Nudes,
Florence, Uffizi, Cabinet of Drawings and Prints

FLORENCE, Uffizi (no. 241)
Pietà

tempera on parchment glued onto wood (14 3/4 × 9 7/8 in.) Sakcinski identified it as the painting which Clovio did for Duke Cosimo I de'Medici in Florence, 1553, and remembered by Vasari: *"For the said Lord Duke, Don Clovio did ... a small painting of a pietà of which we have the drawing ..."* To the pathos of Michelangelesque inspiration are added the entranced fixedness of the characters and the cut treatment of the outlines results from the vicinity of Bronzino's works. There is a transcribed engraving (A. A. I. Suppl. rel.) of this *Pietà* by Lavino the younger, in the Bibliotheque Nationale, Paris.

Bibliography

G. VASARI, 1550 and 1568, ed. 1965, VII, p. 447; I. SAKCINSKI, 1852, p. 52; J. W. BRADLEY, 1891 and 1971, p. 352; M. LEVI D'ANCONA, 1950, p. 67; G. MUZZIOLI, 1953, p. 496; M. CIONINI-VISANI 1971, p. 136. ill. 183.

FLORENCE, Uffizi, Cabinet of Drawings and Prints (no. 1488 E)
An Armed Mounted Soldier Slaying Two Nudes
bistre and black pen on paper (12 1/2 × 10 1/2 in.)

It is not signed. The parallel and sharp outline is not common to Clovio, but the beautiful drawing certainly belongs to his hand. The impetuous line delineates, with insistence, the musculature of the nudes on the ground and acquires particular energy in the image of the horse. This was probably a preparatory study for a detail of a *Conversation of Saint Paul*, and is very near to the drawing of the same subject in the British Museum, London (no. 1946-7-13-322), and is therefore to be placed at about 1570.

Bibliography

P. N. FERRI, 189, p. 330.

FLORENCE, Uffizi, Cabinet of Drawings and Prints (no. 15562 F)

Christ Carrying the Cross
white-lead pencil and black charcoal on paper (5 3/4 × 8 1/2 in.)

Previously thought to be by Penni, it was orally attributed to Clovio by Ph. Poncey (1965). The drawing is finished, soft, shaded and intensely pathetic.
Unpublished

FLORENCE, Uffizi, Cabinet of Drawings and Prints (no. 2457 F)

Deposition
black pencil on paper (3 1/4 × 1 1/2 in.)

Abrasions at the corners and marks all over the sheet. The drawing is unsigned and to be attributed to Clovio's hand as it is very near, the variations being minimal to the *Deposition* at toe Art Institute of Chicago (no. 223173) and to the signed *Deposition* at the British Museum, London (no. 1895-9-654). Like these it is to be related to the mature period of Clovio's activity after 1540.
Unpublished

LONDON, British Museum (MS. ADD. 20927)

The Stuart de Rothesay Book of Hours

The codex, which consists of 172 sheets of parchment of 5 1/4 × 3 1/2 in each, corresponds with the *Beatissimae Virginis Mariae Officium,* written by Bartolomeo Sanvito and bought by the British Museum in 1835 from Lord Stuart de Rothesay. In the lower margin of fo. 14r it bears the red and green vertical bands of Cardinal Grimani's coat of arms, for whom, according to Vasari, it was decorated by Giulio Clovio in Perugia between 1534 and 1537/38. In fact, Vasari says "*In Perugia with the Cardinal . . . he got him to illuminate an Office of Our Lady with four beautiful stories*". Only fo. 172 with the scene of the *Angel and Tobias* does not correspond with the scene of Vasari's text where he remembers only four miniatures, but it is possible to advance the hypothesis, by reason of the insipid coloring, the modest ornamentation and very theme itself which is in substance extraneous to that of the *Officium Virginis,* that the fifth miniature is a later addition. The pages face each other and are paired as follows:

fo. 13 v. *The Annunciation with a rich border.*

fo. 14 r. The words BEATISSIME/VIRGINIS MA/RIE OFFICIUM/AD MATUTINUM/VERSUS. DOMINE LA/BIA MEA APERIS/ET OS MEUM/ are within a rich border. In the initial "D" of Domine there is a colored miniature with the Madonna and Child.
The borders of the two sheets, although differing in their single elements, are both symmetrically laid out, the first on a yellow background and the second on a pale blue, and both engraved in gold. At the top center of each border there is a mask, and towards the external margins two gilded baskets, the one full of fruit the other of flowers and supported by robust putti. Under these figures there are two cameos, one of the *Presentation at the Temple* (fo. 13) and the other the *Adoration of the Kings* (fo. 14). On the lower border of fo. 13 two nude putti are holding a cameo with the *Nativity,* which in the lower border of fo. 14 r corresponds with a garland of fruit and leaves and the Grimani coat-of-arms also held by two robust cupids.

Christ Carrying the Cross,
Florence, Uffizi, Cabinet of Drawings and Prints

Deposition,
Florence, Uffizi, Cabinet of Drawings and Prints

fo. 91 v. *David Praying* with a rich border.

fo. 92 r. The words INCIPIUNT SEP/TEM PSALMI PE/NITENTIALES AN/TIPHONA. NE RE/MINI-SCARIS. PSALMUS/DOMINE NE/ FURORE TUO/ ARGUAS ME: NEO// are within a rich border. In the initial "D" there is a beautiful illuminated head of an old man.

The exquisitely worked and elegant borders of the two pages are full of trophies, armour, cuirasses, helmets and putti, in the upper corners there are virile nudes in the manner of the Sistine Chapel. In the center left-hand border of fo. 19 v. a chiaroscuro cameo showing *Esther before Ahasuerus* corresponds to a cameo in the center right-hand border of fo. 92 r. showing *The Unction of David*. In the lower margins there is a beautiful scene with *David and Goliath* (fo. 91 v.) deriving from the Sistine Chapel, and a *Battle between Skeletons* (fo. 92 r.). fo. 119 v. *Christ at Lazarus' Tomb with Mary and Martha* within a rich border.

fo. 12 r. There are the words INCIPIT OFFICIUM/ MORTUORUM/AD VESPEROS/ANTIPHONA PLA/CEBO DOMINO PSALMUM/DILEXI/QUONIAM EXAU/DIET DOMINUS/. In the initial "D" of Domino is Lazarus's head.

With a splendid effect a background of gold is used in the borders of both of the pages. The greater part of the ornaments derive from the Vatican Loggias. In the center of each lateral border, to the left of fo. 119 v. and to the right of fo. 120 r., there is a cameo with the figure of a lion devouring a deer. At the rest of the two borders two tall satyrs surrounded by birds and monkeys are to be found. The lower margins each contain a rectangular miniature showing a *Battle Between Skeletons and Knights* (fo. 119 v.) and *Some Figures Weeping around a Bier* (fo. 120 r.) fo. 165 v. *The Crucifixion* within a rich border.

fo. 165 v. *The Crucifixion* within a rich border.

fo. 166 r. There are the words INCIPIT.OFFICIU/ SANCTE CRUCIS/AD MATUTINUM/VER + SI-CULUS/DOMINE LABIA MEA APERIES ET OS MEUM ANNU/CIABIT LAUDEM TUA.DEUS within a rich border. Inside the initial "D" there is an illuminated head of Christ crowned with thorns.

On a violet and brown background arabesques, masks and candelabra form the elements of the borders. In the center of each outside border, to the left on fo. 165 v. and to the right on fo. 166 r, there are two lozenge-shaped cameos the former showing *Christ in the Garden of Gethsemane*, and the latter the *Resurrection*. Two rectangular scenes in gilded chiaroscuro form the lower margins, representing *The Way of the Cross* (fo. 165 v.) and the *Descent of Christ into Limbo* (fo. 166 r.).

Bibliography

G. VASARI, 1550 and 1568, ed. 1965, p. 442; BRITISH MUSEUM, 1854/60, p. 293—294; J. W. BRADLEY, 1891 and 1971, p. 304—311; J. A. HEBERT, 1911, p. 305; SOCIETA FRANCESE DI RIPRODUZIONE DEI MANOSCRITTI, 1914/20, II, p. 120; BRITISH MUSEUM, 1928, IV. p. 17—18; M. LEVI D'ANCONA, 1950, p. 57; M. CIONINI-VISANI, 1971, p. 125—126, ill. 165, 166, 167.

LONDON, Soane Museum (MS. 11)
Commentary on the Epistle of Saint Paul to the Romans

This consists of 130 pages of parchment and contains the *Commentary on the Epistle to the Romans by Saint Paul* of Cardinal Marino Grimani, for whom it was illuminated-maybe in Perugia-by Clovio between 1534 and 1537/38. It was most likely taken to England by Joseph Smith, the British consul in Venice from 1740 to 1760. It was bought by Sir John Soane in 1833. Each page measures (16 7/8 × 12 7/8).

fo. 1. A rich border frames the beginning of the text. The title *"Marini Grimani Veneti S.R.E. Cardinalis et patriarchae Aquileiae. Epistola in commentarios epistolarum pauli"* is in a panel. The text begins with initial "I" in dark gold, formed by a beautiful ancient Roman figure standing upright. The greater part of the elements in the border derive from the Vatican Loggias. We notice a small medallion with a profile head of *Minerva*, which corresponds with a splendid drawing in Windsor Castle (no. 243). In the oposite margin to the left there are Raphaelesque *Three Graces* within a small cuspidated panel. The figure of the old woman with the distaff in the bottom left could be understood as Ceres. The lower margin is completed by a beautiful landscape.

fo. 8 v. *The Conversion of Saint Paul* full page.

It is an adaption from Raphael's cartoon of the same subject, and drawn between 1515 and 1516 for a tapestry for the Sistine Chapel. In 1521 the cartoon was in Venice in the house of Cardinal Domenico Grimani, uncle to Marino, probably his heir, where Marcantonio Michiel saw it and noted: *"the large cartoon of the "Conversion of Saint Paul" by the hand of Raphael, which had served for one of the tapestries of the Chapel ..."*. The images in the borders are somewhat rich: Michelangelesque nudes twist and turn in the upper corners, while in the lower left is the figure of Venus-Peace with the torch upside-down. In the center of each border is a cameo: to the top in gilded chiaroscuro the *Trinity*, in the center of the right-hand border the figure of *Saint Paul* also in gilded chiaroscuro, in the center of the left-hand border a cameo with a miniature of *Saint Paul Preaching to the Athenians* deriving from Raphael's cartoon with the *Sacrifice to Lystra*, at the bottom a miniature in a frame repeats Giulio Romano's *Stoning of Saint Stephen*. The rest is thick with arms, cuirasses, trophies and at the bottom with putti. In a little bronze plaque placed obliquely in the bottom right there is written MARINO/GRIMA/SUO IULIUS/CROVATA/PINGEBA/T.

fo. 9 Containing the title and the beginning of the *Commentary*. Four cameos are in the central points of the borders: at the top in the interior of a study two gentlemen are standing in front of a person sitting at a table, the cameo to the left has a standing figure with the words "PASTORIS MUNUS", in the center of the right border is an oval with the portrait of the patron cardinal; at the bottom in a circle a group of putti are holding up the shield and the coat of arms of the Grimani, over which a winged putto holds the cardinal's hat. On either side of the cameo in the top margin are two doves holding a ribbon with the words SIMP/LICES, which corresponds with, in the lower margin, two dragons on whose feet is a ribbon with the words PRU/DE/N/TES, according to the Christian motto *"Prudente come il serpente, semplice come la colomba"*. As in fo. 8 v., athletic nudes fill the upper corners of the border, while in the bottom right the figure of Mars-War corresponds to that of Venus-Peace on the preceding sheet. In the interior of the page is a wide landscape, at the sides of which stand two elegantly draped women representing Faith and Pity. Two putti hold a large plaque on which one reads MARINI GRIMANI VENETI/SRE CARDINALIS/ET PATRIARCHAE/AQUILEIAE N EPISTOLAM PAULI/AD ROMANOS COMMEN/TARIORUM CAP. PRIMUM.
Under the capital letters the word PAVLUS.

Bibliography

G. VASARI, 1550 and 1568, ed. 1965, VII, p. 442; M. MICHIEL (Anonymos Morellian), 1884, p. 200; G. F. WAAGEN, 1850, p. 326; J. W. BRADLEY, 1891 and 1971, p. 244—253; E. G. MILLAR, 1914/1920, p. 116—128; M. LEVI D'ANCONA, 1950, p. 71; J. SUMMERSON, 1951, February; M. CIONINI-VISANI, 1971, p. 126, ill. 168, 169.

Crucifixion,
London, British Museum, Print Room

LONDON, British Museum, Print Room (no. 1860-6-16-19)
Crucifixion
black charcoal on paper (11 × 8 7/8 in.)

The unsigned drawing is to be attributed to Clovio for its unmistakable stylistic references. It is very close to the illuminated etching by Cornelis Cort (London, British Museum, Print Room, no. 1895-9-15-1407) transcribed by Clovio, as the inscription at the bottom left states *"don Julio Clovio de Croatia invenit"*, and which it minutely repeats with only the addition of the figure of Mary Magdalen at the foot of the cross, as it appears in the Uffizi *Crucifixion* (no. 812).
The scene is symmetrically constructed. The robust, austere figures, dressed in roomy garments, are drawn with a generous hand and are chiaroscuroed.

Deposition,
London, British Museum, Print Room

LONDON, British Museum, Print Room
(no. 1895-9-15-654)
Deposition
black pen and bistre on paper (9 7/8 × 8 3/8 in.)

Signed *"don Juilio Clovio f.".* The drawing is light
and very soft. The closed construction of the group
within an ideal circular line, the heavy pathos of the
characters show once again Michelangelo's influence
on Clovio. Very near to the *Deposition* (no. 2457) of
the Uffizi, Florence, and of that of the Art Institute
of Chicago this drawing belongs to Clovio's mature
period.

Bibliography

M. CIONINI-VISANI, 1971; p. 137, fig. 184, p. 143,
no. 70.

LONDON, British Museum, Print Room
(no. 1946-7-13-322)
Conversion of Saint Paul
ink and brown water-colour, heightened with white-
lead on paper (10 5/8 × 17 3/8 in.)

The characters which crowd the scene are divided into
two groups by the figure of a soldier, with a shield
on his shoulders, running to help Saint Paul who,
dazzled, is being supported by a nude. The impetuous
and emphatic drawing must have been a study for a
Conversion of Saint Paul some thirty years before the
one included in the Soane codex, (fo. 8 v.).
Many engravings derive from this work (Florence,
Uffizi, Cabinet of Drawings and Prints) and an oil
painting on copper by Bartolomeo Sprangher (Milan,
Pinacoteca Ambrosiana), catalogued under the name
of Clovio.

Conversion of Saint Paul,
London, British Museum, Print Room

Bibliography

A. RATTI, 1907, p. 52; G. GALBIATI, 1951, p. 133;
M. CIONINI-VISANI, 1971, p. 126 fig. 171,172.

MILAN, private collection
Deposition
tempera on parchment (9 3/8 × 6 7/8 in)

The miniature, unknown until it appeared in the
Mostra dell' Arredamento del Cinquecento (Vicenza
1973), is to be attributed to Clovio for the technique,
the style (the briliant and acid colors, the receding
perspective are typical), and the soft and pathetic
feeling which also places the work in the artist's later
years.
The same collector possesses a drawing which closely
resembles the miniature (the woman seen from the
back in the foreground is missing) and is referable to
the German School of around 1620. Also Prof. Grgo
Gamulin mentions a painting of the same subject (Zagreb, Strossmayerova Galerija), referred by him to
Giovanni Battista Maganza, and which minutely repeats Clovio's miniature. For all three of the examples
it is necessary to think of a common prototype, not
as yet identified.

Bibliography

CATALOG Mostra dell'Arredamento del Cinquecento,
Vicenza 1973, p. 29.

Judith Putting the Head of Holofernes in her Bag,
Zagreb, Graf. kabinet Jugoslavenske akademije nauka

91

MILAN, Stanza del Borgo, formerly at Warsaw, Dobrowsky Coll.

Crucifixion (detail)

watered seppia and brushstroke in ink on linted paper (16 1/8 × 11 1/8 in)

The drawing, caried out in an open and sketchy manner, represents a subtle interpretation of a detail of Michelangelo's fresco of the "Crucifixion of Saint Paul", painted in the Paoline Chapel between 1542 and 1550. Therefore the drawing is to be dated in the second half of the century, in a moment of intense Michelangelesque influence.

Bibliography

CATALOG Disegni Italiani e Stranieri del '500 e '600 Stanza del Borgo, Milan 1969, p. 42—43.

NEW YORK, Public Library (MS. 91)

Towneley Lectionary

tempera on parchment (19 × 12 7/8 in)

The work of various artists, among whom Clovio who illuminated four large full-page scenes, numbers 5v., 6v., 16v., 23v.

The dating of Clovio's miniatures is somewhat controversial: Bradley (1891 and 1971, p. 351) proposes 1546, A. E. Bye (1917, p. 88—89) thinks of the years from 1531 to 1540, Levi D'Ancona believes sheets 6v, and 23v, to have been illuminated before 1568 as they are both mentioned in the second edition of Vasari's Lives, and between 1568 and 1577 for sheets 5v. and 16v. as they figure in the inventory laid down by Clovio himself in 1577. The most convincing proposal is W. Smith's (1955), according to whom the Lectionary was all illuminated between 1550 and 1560; this dating could even be restricted to the years 1550/1556 (during these years Clovio was Ottavio Farnese's guest at Parma), and find confirmation in the collaboration — on fo. 23v. — between Clovio and Peter Brueghel, present in Rome in 1553.

fo. 5v. Nativity.

The figures are placed around the group of the Holy Family, at the center of architectual ruins, in disconnected groups, while in a vortex of light angels fly above. The gilded chiaroscuro borders repeat the usual motifs, though simplified, of the Soane codex and of the Morgan codex. At the foot of the page are garlands of flowers and fruit and gilded chiaroscuro medallions of the Circumcision, The Adoration of the Kings and the Presentation at the Temple. Cardinal Farnese's coat of arms is at the center of the lower border.

fo. 6v. The Calling of the Apostles.

Andrew, Judas, James and John are before the sitting Christ, the other Apostles are behind Him, with a back-ground of classical architecture. The gilded chiaroscuro borders are decorated with colossal flesh-coloured caryatids draped in colored materials an a blue background. Bradley (1891 and 1971, p. 256) does not consider this to be by Clovio's hand.

fo. 16v. Resurrection.

The uncovered tomb in the center with Christ rising to the heavens, the soldiers stand around in surprise and fear. The somewhat sober borders are in gilded chiaroscuro; the lower one has two rectangular scenes with The Marys at the Sepulchre and Christ Appearing before Mary Magdalen.

fo. 23v. The Last Judgement.

This is considered Clovio's masterpiece. Vasari writes: "The Last Judgement so beautiful, in fact wonderful and marvellous, that I am confused when thinking of it, and maintain that one cannot, I will not say do, but see, or imagine, an even more beautiful miniature." All the material for a large fresco is contained within the reduced dimensions of the illuminated page. At the center top the Saviour holds the cross and the cherubs crowd around, below angels in different attitudes blow the trumpets of judgement. Higher up are innumerable saints, martyrs and confessors. On the frame of a gilded gold tone, and rich in gold relief are sculptured nudes in various attitudes. In a small rectangular frame (1 5/8 × 2 7/8 in) at the center of the lower margin is the Battle between Sailing-ships, in which De Tolnay (1965, p. 113) recognized the hand of Peter Brueghel. There is a reminder of Clovio's collaboration with the Flemish master also in the inventory of Clovio's personal possessions, published by Bertolotti (1882, p. 11): "A small miniature half done by his hand (Clovio's) and the other half by Maestro Pietro Brugole's".

Bibliography

G. VASARI, 1550/1568, ed. 1965, VII, 449; G. BAGLIONE, 1644, p. 15; M. A. BERTOLOTTI, 1882, p. 11; J. X. BRADLEY, 1891 and 1971, p. 254—260; A. B. BYE, 1917 February, p. 88—99; M. Levi D'ANCONA, 1950, p. 57—74; W. SMITH, 1955 (unpublished); Ch. DE TOLNAY, March, p. 110—114; M. CIONINI-VISANI, 1971, p. 137—138, ill. 185, 186, 187, 191.

NEW YORK, Pierpont Morgan Library (MS. 69)

Farnese Book of Hours or Officium Virginis

Written by Francesco Monterchi and illuminated in Rome from 1537 to 1546 by Giulio Clovio for Cardinal Alessandro Farnese, the codex arrived, by a series of inheritances, to Alfonso di Borbone, Count of Caserta, from whom it was bought in 1903 through the mediation of J. Goldschmidt. "Iulius Clovius Macedo Monumenta Haec Alexandro Farnesio Cardinali Suo Domino faciebat MDXLV" is written in the medallion on the last page. The decoration consists of twenty-eight pages with scenes from the Old and New Testament, besides two scenes of liturgic events of XV cent. on adjoining pages. With exception of these latter, all of the miniatures are contained within wonderful complicated borders. There are also thirty-five frames, containing the text, illuminated with a great variety and wealth of motifs. Throughout the codex Clovio appears as a very sensitive and original interpreter of Michelangelo's style and of the Roman manner, besides remembering the Grimani Evangelistery (Venice, Marciana Library).

Each page measures (6 7/8 × 4 1/4 in)

fo. 4v. Annunciation.

The angel with large, soft wings glides before the Virgin who is kneeling beside a reading desk. Behind them a window opens onto a landscape with a classical temple. In the center of the lower border there are the Farnese coat of arms surmounted by cardinal's hat, and putti with garlands of flowers to the right and to the left. In the left border there is a cloaked female figure (a sibyl?) in a niche.

fo. 5. The Prophecy of the Birth of Christ to King Achaz.

To the left Isaiah is sitting, holding a tablet. Achaz, the King of Judea, is standing before him. There is an old man behind Isaiah and to his right an angel pointing to the sky. In the right-hand border there is the figure of a woman (a sibyl?) in a niche, as in fo. 4v.

fo. 6v. and 7. The only border is in the lower margin of the two pages, it shows a vast landscape with a lake or a river strewn with islands, with birds of paradise flying over it. There are also two panels of grotesques, one to the left of fo. 6v., and the other to the right of fo. 7.

fo. 9v. and 10. On each page there is a candelabrum with cameos and grotesques in the style of the Vatican Logge.

92

fo. 11v. and 12. A panel of grotesques on each page. At the center of the panel to the left (fo. 11v.) there is a medallion with a building on a rock, and at the center of the panel to the right (fo. 12) a landscape with trees.

fo. 17v. *The Visitation.*

Mary and Elizabeth meet on a background of hills and classic buildings. In the gilded border there are little colored cameos, in the one in the center of the lower margin there is the scene of the *Virgin Climbing the Temple Steps.*

fo. 18. *Justice and Peace Embracing.*

A temple is in the background. Behind Justice are two putti, one holding a helmet, the other a sword; behind Peace are three putti with garlands of laurel and cornucopia. The gilded border corresponds to that of fo. 17v., with the *Marriage of the Virgin* in a small cameo in the center of the lower margin.

fo. 20v. and 21. A wide view of the *Bay of Naples* occupies the lower margin of both pages. To the extreme left are two panels decorated with grotesques under each of which stands a knight pompously dressed in an oriental manner.

fo. 26v. *Adoration of the Shepherds.*

Three painted cameos are in the border among nude and semi-nude figures, and putti, at the center top *Angels around the Crib,* center bottom *Christ Among the Elders,* and center left a *Putto Astride a Dolphin.*

fo. 27. *Temptation.*

Adam and Eve in Eden. Three cameos are in the border among nude and semi-nude figures, and putti; at the center top the *Creation of Eve,* center right *Pegasus* and center bottom the *Expulsion from Eden.*

fo. 28.v. and 29. Medallions with boards and leopards in the borders.

fo. 30v. *The Annunciation to the Shepherds.*

Nude female figures and putti with garlands are in the border.

fo. 31. *The Prophecy of the Birth of Christ to the Emperor Augustus.*

The sibyl Tiburtine shows the Virgin and Child in the sky to the kneeling Augustus. In the border there are male and female nudes and putti with garlands, as in fo. 30v.

fo. 32v. and 33. A landscape of trees takes up the lower margins of both pages. In the background the nude figure of a man seems to be running away from an eruption, in the foreground a river god points to the entrance of a cave. In an oval medallion in the left-hand border (fo. 32v.) is a head of *Alexander the Great,* which corresponds to an oval medallion, in the center of the right-hand border (fo. 33), with the probable portrait of *Cardinal Alessandro Farnese;* below this, Peace holds up a papal tiara.

fo. 34v. *The Circumcision.*

Among the people that crowd the marble colonnade "... *Pope Paul III is portrayed for Simon, and behind the scene the portraits of Mancina and Settimia, Roman gentlewomen, who were of great beauty ...*" (Vasari, ed. 1965, VII, p. 444). The gilded monochrome borders are made up with two large caryatids, putti and cameos.

fo. 35. *The Baptism of Christ.*

The scene is accompanied by a group of bathers, who, in their poses, remind one of the figures in Michelangelo's *Battle of Casina.* The border in gilded monochrome is formed, as in fo. 34v, with two large caryatids, putti and cameos.

fo. 38v. *Adoration of the Kings.*

In the border, in color, two large nudes and putti are placed on the gilded monochrome of the frame.

fo. 39. *The Meeting Between King Solomon and the Queen of Sheba.*

The characters crowd into an ambience of Raphaelesque origin. In the bottom left-hand corner a dwarf, perhaps a portrait, looks out towards the spectator.

fo. 40v. and 41. *The Feast of Testaccio.*

The representation of the event fills the lower margin of two joining pages. This miniature was also remembered by Vasari "... *within this at the foot, and carried out in figures no bigger than ants, is the whole feast of Testaccio, and it is a miraculous thing for looking at ...*" (ed. 1965, VII, p. 444—445)

fo. 42v. *Flight into Egypt.*

Two angels on foot follow the Virgin's ride. In the background Gaius Cestius' Pyramid and Saint Paul's Gate. In the borders precious stones and pearl necklaces aternate with small putti in different poses.

fo. 43. *The Crossing of the Red Sea.*

In the background, to the left, the children of Israel are camping on the shores of the Red Sea, in the foreground Moses is leading them across the sea. The border repeats the motifs of the adjoining page.

fo. 46v. In the lateral left border there are Pompeian motifs and a long oval medallion with *Cardinal Alessandro Farnese in Prayer.*

fo. 47. In the lateral right border, which repeats the Pompeian motifs of the left (fo. 46v.), is a long oval medallion with the *Virgin in Prayer,* probably the portrait of Pope Paul III's daughter *Lucretia Farnese.*

fo. 48v. *The Coronation of the Virgin.*

In the gilded monochrome borders are two large caryatids in the form of hooded old men. In the center of the lower margin is a cameo with the *Death of the Virgin.*

fo. 49. *Esther Crowned by Ahasuerus.*

Standing on the steps, to the left, and facing outwards, is a young *Prince* with a sword, maybe the portrait of Ottavio Farnese. The border repeats that of the opposite page.

fo. 50v. and 51. A fantastic view of *Island of Tiberina* fills the lower margins of the two facing pages. The bust of the Emperor Augustus, the figure of Mars with helmet, cuirass and shield, and Apollo with a lyre follow one another on a panel in the left-hand lateral margin ((fo. 50v.). In the right-hand lateral margin (fo. 51) are found a bust of Julius Caesar, the figure of Minerva with a helmet and shield and that of Pan with his reed-pipe.

fo. 54v. In the outside margin, carried out in light Pompeian motifs, there is a long oval cameo with the *Angel* of the Annunciation.

fo. 55. In the border of the outside margin is a long oval, with the *Virgin Mary* on a dark ground, corresponding to the *Angel* of the preceding page.

fo. 59v. *The Creation.*

The Creator closely repeats the image of *God the Father* in the *Creation of the Planets* of the Sistine Chapel. In the background is the kneeling *Virgin.* The frame, in gilded monochrome, appears somewhat simplified in respect to the preceding ones. In El Greco's *Portrait of Clovio* (Naples, Capodimonte), the *Officium Virginis,* which the miniaturist holds in his hand, is open at this page.

fo. 60. *The Holy Family.*

The Virgin, holding the Infant Christ, is in front of a hut, and Saint Joseph is leaning on a stick in the background. The simple border repeats that of the adjoining page.

fo. 61v. and 62. There is a *View with Towers and Bridges* in lower margins of the two facing pages.

fo. 63v. *The Death of Uriah.*

A battle scene. In the foreground Uriah lies dead beside his horse.

fo. 64. *David in Prayer.*

David prays in an interior with his harp on the floor beside him. In the complex gilded monochrome border there are two figures of Venus in natural colors, seen from the back.

fo. 66v. and 67. A fantastic view with *Sicily with Etna* is in the lower margin of the two adjoining pages. Candelabra in the style of the Vatican Loggias, similar to those of fo. 1 of the Soane *Commentary* are in the outside margins.

fo. 72v. and 73. Litany with the Corpus Christi Day Procession "... he then carried out in very minute figures the procession which takes place in Rome to celebrate Corpus Christi Day, full of officials with the torches, bishops and cardinals, and the Holy Sacrament carried by the Pope, with the rest of the court and the guards of lancers..." (Vasari, ed 1965, VIII, p. 445). To the left is a view of the old Basilica of Saint Peter, and to the right the Castle of Sant'Angelo. At the top, on fo. 72v., the *Trinity*, on fo. 73, *The Virgin Mary Supported by Saints and Martyrs.*

fo. 79v. *The Triumph of Death.*

Death enthroned has a multitude of corpses at his feet. The border consists of two large hooded figures and of putti leaning on a skull in the upper margin and of a sarcophagus in the lower one.

fo. 80. *The Resurrection of Lazarus.*

Lazarus is being taken out of the tomb by two men. A Bramantesque temple is in the background. The border repeats that of the preceding page.

fo 86v. and 87. *A Battle between Skeletons and Knights.*

The scene takes up the lower margin of the adjoining pages. In the middle of the lateral margins two heads of old people face each other from chiaroscuro cameos, underneath are two full-length hooded figures.

fo 90v. and 91. *Fantastic View.*

A lake landscape scattered with islands fills the lower margins of the two adjoining pages. The outer margins are decorated with motifs of grotesques and with two busts of Diana of Ephesus.

fo. 102v. *Crucifixion.*

With some variations the scene repeats the drawing of the British Museum (no 1860-6-16-19). In the borders putti alternate with robust nudes of old men from whose hands ribbons unfurl. In a rectangular frame in the middle of the lower margin *Christ Appears to the Apostles.*

fo. 103. *The Bronze Serpent.*

At the top the Children of Israel support the dying Aaron, while in the foreground some are fighting and drawing near to the serpent while others stare at the rod with the bronze serpent. The scene comes practically straight from the Sistine Chapel, where Michelangelo painted the same subject. The borders are very similar to those of the preceding page, only the two nude caryatids are facing the opposite way. Within a rectangular frame at the bottom center is the *Resurrection.*

fo. 104v. and 105. *The Tower of Babel* and *A Landscape of Mountains* are in the lower margins of the two adjoining pages. In the side margins are two

The Holy Family with Saint Elizabeth and Other Figures, New York, Wildenstein Foundation

panels with motifs of grotesques, putti and the image of *Fame.*

fo. 106v. *The Pentecost.*

The characters are crowded into an interior with strongly emphatic poses. Virile and female nudes, and little putti alternate in the rich gilded chiaroscuro borders.

fo. 107. *The Building of the Tower of Babel.*

The scene closely repeats fo. 206 of the *Grimani Evangelistery* (Venice, Marciana Library). With the minimum of variations the margins repeat the decorations of the preceding page.

fo. 108v. At the bottom a view of the old *Saint Peter's Basilica.* The full figure of Saint Peter is in an oval medallion in the middle of the left margin.

fo. 109. At the bottom a view of *Roman Ruins with an Obelisk.* The Tiburtine Sibyl is in an oval medallion in the center right margin.

fo. 111v. and 112. In the side margins are two ovals with full figures on a dark ground. At the bottom two medallions with Pompeian "scherzi".

Bibliography

G. VASARI, 1550/1568, ed. 1965, VII, p. 443—446; G. BAGLIONE, 1644, p. 15; I SAKCINSKI, 1852, p. 18—19, 42—47, 74; W. BRADLEY, 1887, I. no. 8, p. 237; J. M. BRADLEY, 1891 and 1971, p. 270—274, A. E. BYE, 1917, V, p. 97—99; M. LEVI D'ANCONA, 1950, July Sept., p. 55; M. HAARSEN-G. K. BOYCE, 1953, no. 102; W. SMITH, 1955, unpublished; W. SMITH, 1964, p. 395/401; M. CIONINI-VISANI, 1971, p. 130—135, ill. 175, 176, 177, 178, 179, 180, 181, 182.

NEW YORK, Wildenstein Foundation
The Holy Family with Saint Elizabeth and Other Figures
tempera on parchment (8 3/4 × 6 in)

Datable in the second half of the sixth decade of the XVI cent., it could be one of the four miniatures which were given to the Escorial by Philip II in 1574 and from there taken by Napoleon's troops in 1808. The Escorial inventory for the years 1571 to 1598 lists at number 1518 a *Holy Family with Saint Elizabeth, Saint John and Saint Joseph*, previously belonging to Ruy Gomez de Silva, Philip II's favourite, and Vasari remembers: *"For the same Cardinal Farnese he did a painting of Our Lady with her Son in her arms, Saint Elizabeth, Saint John and other figures, which was sent to Spain to Rigomes"*. A *"small painting by Don Julio"* sent by Cardinal Farnese to Ruy Gomez is mentioned in a letter, dated December 4th, 1556, and addressed to Cardinal Giuliano Ardinghelli, the Duke of Parma's Ambassador at the Court of Brussels, and who was also commissioned to deliver the miniature. It is possible that it refers in fact to this miniature but there is no other evidence to establish it with certainty. Levi D'Ancona (1950) proposes dating the work between 1560 and 1561. thereby excluding its possible identification with the one given to Ruy Gomez.

Bibliography

G. VASARI, 1550 and 1568, ed. 1965, VII, p. 446; F. BORMIAN BERMEJO, 1820, p. 300—301; A. RONCHINI 1865, p. 262; J. W. BRADLEY, 1891 and 1971, p. 388—389; J. ZARCO CUEVAS, 1930, p. 96; M. LEVI D'ANCONA, 1950, p. 58—62; M. CIONINI-VISANI, 1971, p. 138 and 143, note 77.

NEW YORK, Wildenstein Foundation
The Holy Family with an Armed Figure
tempera on parchment (6 7/8 × 4 1/8 in)

Datable at around 1553. The head of the armed figure recalls the beautiful illuminated profile portrait of Alexander the Great in the *Farnese Book of Hours* (fo. 32v.) and in the drawing in Windsor Castle (no. 243) — this latter with some variations. As Levi D'Ancona suggested, the ephebic head could be thought to represent the very young Alessandro Farnese, for whose family the miniature could have been done.

Bibliography

M. LEVI D'ANCONA, 1950, p. 73; M. CIONINI-VISANI, 1971, p. 138.

NEW YORK, Wildenstein Foundation
David and Goliath
tempera on parchment (11 1/2 × 8 1/4 in)

Done for Margherita Farnese around 1560, and given by Philip II of Spain to Escorial and from there removed by Napoleon's troops in 1808. Vasari remembers *"a representation where David cuts the head of the giant Goliath, it was given by the same Cardinal (Farnese) to Madame Margharita of Austria, who sent it to her brother King Philip together with another where Judith cuts Holofernes's head"*. Therefore the miniature with *David and Goliath* was "pendant" to the other, which was spoken of in the letter to Mar-

The Holy Family with an Armed Figure,
New York, Wildenstein Foundation

David and Goliath,
New York, Wildenstein Foundation

The Miracle of the Serpents,
New York, Schwab Gallery

gherita of Austria and dated 11th September 1561. The
inventory of Escorial, from 1571 to 1598, lists (no.
1517) *"Un quadro pequeno de madona, illuminado de
mano de don Julio: la Historia de David quando mato
el gigante Golias..."* In his *Description de El Escorial*,
1626, Cassiano Dal Pozzo notes *"... in a little room
where there were various relics...: among the small
paintings that I saw worthy of consideration were
three very beautiful ones by the hand of Don Giulio
Clovio, no bigger than the palm of the hand usually,
they were very diligent miniatures on parchment"*. One
of the three miniatures could have been this one.
The miniature, which derives from a painting of *David
and Goliath* by Daniele da Volterra (Paris, Louvre),
has pale cold colors among which blue is dominant.

Bibliography

G. VASARI, 1550 and 1568, ed. 1965, VII, p. 447;
F. BORMIAN BERMEJO, 1820, p. 300—301; I.
SACKINSKI, 1852, p. 48; J. W. BRADLEY, 1891
and 1971, p. 354; J. ZARCO CUEVAS, 1930, p. 96;
M. LEVI D'ANCONA, 1950, p. 58—63; C. DAL
POZZO, 1972, p. 21; M. CIONINI-VISANI, 1971, p.
138;

NEW YORK, Schwab Gallery
The Miracle of the Serpents
black pen and bistre on paper (17 1/8 × 15 7/8 in)

The group of the guards was drawn on a separate
piece of paper and then struck onto the sheet. The
technique *"a puntini"* with a lot of shading is that
typical one of Michelangelo's later drawings and is
often used by Giulio Clovio, as one can notice in the
Consignment of the Keys (Windsor Castle, no. 244)
and in *The Virgin with Child, Saint John and Saint
Joseph* (Windsor Castle, no. 242). In the inventory of
Clovio's possessions of 1577, published by Bertolotti,
there is a *"Story of the Serpents, in pen, copied by
Don Giulio and invented by Maestro Michelangelo"*.
On the basis of such evidence and because of the
obvious affinity in style, the drawing (which shows the
moment when Aaron's rod, cast before Pharaoh, turns
into a serpent), is to be placed in the catalog of drawings appertaining to Clovio's mature period.

Bibliography

M. A. BERTOLOTTI, 1882, p. 12.

PARIS, LOUVRE, Cabinet of Drawings
(R. F. 3977)
Saint Paul Blinding Elima
tempera on parchment (12 7/8 × 8 7/8 in)

The miniature, which seems very close to the moment of the Soane codex, is a tribute to the Raphael tapestry with *Saint Paul who is Blinding Elima* and therefore does not represent the *Healing of the Blindman* as De La Coste-Messeliere suggests. The sheet is very likely the one remembered by Francisco dé Hollanda: *"... he showed us ... two full pages of a book. On the first there was a miniature with Saint Paul visiting a blindman in the presence of a Roman proconsul..."* The miniature is characterized by an intense and refined chromatic play on the background of grey architecture. One notices above all the figure of the emperor in which the taste for precious and iridescent colours acquires particular relief. It is also interesting to notice the typology of the characters that form the crowd, partly Raphaelesque and partly, especially to the right, presumably drawn from German engravings.

Bibliography
A. M. BESSONE AURELI, introduction to F. DE. HOLLANDA, 1939, p. 192; T. H. COLDING, 1953, p. 68, fig. 104; M. G. DE LA COSTE-MESSELIERE, 1959, no. 52, p. 8; M. CIONINI-VISANI, 1971, p. 131.

PARIS, LOUVRE, Cabinet of Drawings
The Theological Virtues
tempera on parchment (12 7/8 × 8 7/8 in)

This miniature is remembered, together with that of *Saint Paul Blinding Elima* (Louvre, R. F. 3977), by Francisco dé Hollanda: *"... and on the other Charity and various figures between buildings and Corinthian columns... In beauty it beat all of the most valuable that had ever come before my eyes..."* Bessone Aureli suggests that the book, which according to the Portuguese miniaturist both sheets should have come from, could be the *Commentary on the Epistle of Saint Paul*. This is confirmed by the theme of the first sheet (R. F. 3977) and the allegories of the second (R. F. 3978), the great number of Raphaelsque references as well as the presence of the red and black hands of the Grimani family's coat of arms (it is to be remembered that Marino Grimani was the purshaser of the Soane codex). The difference in size between the London codex and the two sheets in Paris can be explained by the lack of the margins in the last two.

Bibliography
A. M. BESSONE AURELI, introduction to F. DE HOLLANDA, 1939, p. 192, note 12; T. H. COLDING, 1953, p. 68, fig. 103; M. G. DE LA COSTE MESSE-LIERE, 1959, no. 52, p. 8; M. CIONINI-VISANI, 1971, p. 130, fig. 177.

PARIS, LOUVRE, Cabinet of Drawings
(no. 3044)
Christ Presenting the Keys to Saint Peter
tempera on parchment (15 1/4 × 11 1/2 in)

Traditionally attributed to Clovio it is to be considered in connection with the drawing of the same subject at Windsor Castle (no. 244), which A. E. Popham cataloged under the name of Giulio Clovio. In both, the figures, organized in the line of an ideal circumference, correspond perfectly, but the background differs, simpler in ther drawing with a fortified city on a hill, developed and complex in the miniature. Here in fact the background becomes an extensive panorama with Minerva's Temple in the Forum of the same name and Trajan's Column, between which there is Noah's Ark surmounted by a construction which does not appear elsewhere. The buildings are in a landscape of harsh and rugged mountains disappearing in the distance with the typical clear blue outlines. The fantastic imagination which combines true and invented elements

reminds one of the numerous landscapes of the *Officium Virginis Farnese* (New York, P. Morgan Library, Ms. 69) and suggests the dating of the sheet at about 1540.

Bibliography
MOREL D'ARLEAUX, V, no. 7600; F. REISET, 1886, no. 198; A. E. POPHAM-J-WILDE, 1949, p. 212, no. 244; F. VIATTE-R. BACOU-G. DELLE PIANE PE-RUGINI, 1973, p. 156, no. 107.

PARIS, LOUVRE, Cabinet of Drawings
(no. 11444)
Deposition
red chalk on paper (15 3/8 × 11 1/8 in)
small marks, a glued tear in the bottom righthand corner

The drawing carries some handwritten notes on the back of the support — on to which it is glued: *"Muziano?"* signed by A. E. Popham and then *"Plutôt dans la direction de Giulio Clovio"* signed by Pouncey. It is to be attributed to the Croatian artists after 1550, when Clovio could have seen Michelangelo's *Pietà* in Florence Cathedral which the drawing recalls both in the iconography and sentiment, stamped with an intense pathos.
Unpublished.

TURIN, Sabauda Gallery, no. 150
The Passion of Christ
tempera on parchment (26 1/8 × 21 7/8 in)

It is formed by four miniatures gathered in a contemporary frame *(The Sermon on the Mount, The Flagellation, The Crucifixion, The Deposition)* cut in the form of an oval which should contain a fifth, today lost.
The attribution to Clovio is traditional: *"The style indirectly re-echoes Raphael and has some resonances of the German engravers"* (Muzzioli, 1953). The surmounting of the highest point of the "manner" induces one to place the work in Clovio's very last years.

Bibliography
G. PACCHIONI, 1932, p. 14, no. 150; G. MUZZIOLI, 1953, p. 495—496; N. GABRIELLI, 1971, p. 108, no. 150, fig. 195; M. CIONINI-VISANI, 1971, p. 140, fig. 190, p. 143, no. 80.

TURIN, Sabauda Gallery, no. 149
The Holy Shroud
water-colour on silk with a linen support
(21 7/8 × 17 1/2 in)

Given to King Vittorio Emanuele II by a Cremona patrician, it became part of the Sabauda Gallery in 1868. Twelve small scenes of the Passion, in blue and gold, frame the central space where there in the Deposition. In a cloud the angels hold the sheet with the impression of the body of Christ. At the top one reads *"The very true portrait of the Holy Sudarium"* and at the bottom, *"OREMUS"*.
The attribution to Clovio is traditional. Notwithstanding the refined workmanship, the miniature appears somewhat conventional, it can be placed in the last period of Clovio's production.

Bibliography
G. PACCHIONI, 1932, p. 14, no. 149; M. G. DE LA COSTEMESSELIERE, 1959, no. 52, p. 9; N. GABRIELLI, 1971, p. 108, no. 149, fig. 194; M. CIONINI-VISANI, p. 140, and 144, no. 81.

TREVISO (Italy) City Library, Ms. 646
The Miracles of the Virgin

Dated 1534, it is a book which tells of the miracles of the Virgin which took place in the Church of Santa Maria Maggiore in Treviso. In the margin above the text of fo. 2 there is written *"Fu cominciato questo libro P. dal Pre'Julio Clovio Can. co Reg. re"* which makes Levi D'Ancona think that not only are the miniature and the pen drawing by Clovio's hand, but also the text.

On fo. the miniature, the colors of which are very damaged (5 1/8 × 6 3/8 in), show the *Madonna and Child* and a monk (maybe even Clovio himself). A pen drawing with *Cupids and Musical Instruments around the Letter "P"* on fo. 26 (4 × 4 1/8 in) is marked "P. Clovio Can. co Reg. re".

Bibliography

M. LEVI D'ANCONA, 1969, p. 197—209; M. CIO-NINI-VISANI, p. 125 and 142, no. 41.

Grimani Evangelistary
VENICE, Marciana Library, lat. I, 103 (11925)
tempera on parchment

The codex consists of a hundred-and-fifty sheets, 11 5/8 × 8 in. each. Dated 1528, it was carried out for Cardinal Marino Grimani, Patriarch of Aquileia, and written by *"presbyter Sebastianus Cavazonus"*. It was bought by the Ministry of Education in 1932 at the auction of the Chester Beatty Collection.

It has numerous ornamented initials, some with embellishments, and twelve miniature with figures of the Evangelists and scenes from the life of Christ. Muzzioli, who distinguishes the work of two artists, does not believe that the miniatures can be attributed to Clovio;

Deposition,
Paris, Louvre, Cabinet of Drawings

Madonna and Child and a Monk,
fo. 2 Miracles of the Virgin, Treviso, Italy, City Library

Cupids and Musical Instruments Around the Letter "P",
fo. 26, Treviso, Italy, City Library

Levi D'Ancona (1950 and 1969), on the other hand, considers them to have been done by Clovio in 1528, when he entered the Monastery of San Ruffino. Though, in effect, believing them to be by Clovio, we propose to distinguish the actual painting of them into two periods: for those in which the influence of the Venetian tradition is more evident between '31 and '34, and around 1538/39 for the *Adoration of the Kings* (fo. lov.) and the *Circumcision* (fo. 9v.) for their strong "Salviatism".

fo. 1r. *Saint Luke Writing* (2 3/4 × 3 1/8 in).
the traditional taste both in the colour and the arrangement gives, on the whole, a modest result. The Grimanis'coat of arms is at the bottom.

fo. 5r. *Nativity* (2 3/4 × 2 3/4 in).
arrangement and color in the Venetian tradition; the weakness of the workmanship makes one think of the intervention of someone else.

fo. 6v. *Saint John* (3 1/8 × 2 3/4 in).
the scene, with a landscape opening and traditional arrangement, is characterized by its strong detachment of color (the red cloak and the green vestment of the Saint).

fo. 9v. *The Circumcision* (2 3/4 × 2 3/4 in).
carried out under the influence of the Roman world and of Northern motifs; on the side there is an embellishment (19,5 cm) in gilded chiaroscuro, on which a cameo with a draped head stands out.

fo. 10v. *Adoration of the Kings* (2 3/4 × 2 3/4 in).
carried out under the influence of the Roman world. On either side of the miniature are identical gilded chiaroscuro embellishments (13 × 13 cm) with a cameo with the images of horsemen.

fo. 52v. *Saint Matthew and the Angel.*
(2 3/4 × 2 3/4 in).
in the traditional Venetian taste, it has warm and strong colors. In the frame with red and blue foliage and putti, is a medallion in *grisaille* with the *Entrance into Jerusalem*.

fo. 85v. *Saint Jerome in his Cell* (2 3/4 × 2 3/4 in).
to the right of the saint a window opens onto a landscape in pale blue tones. A right-angle embellishment (12 × 17 cm) with gold foliage on a deep violet ground is on both sides of the miniature. On the embellishment is a medallion in *grisaille* representing the *Resurrection of Christ* and painted with particular refinement.

fo. 96r. *Saint Mark* (2 3/4 × 2 3/4 in).
the Michelangelesque cut and the very intense expression characterize the figure painted with deep and warm colors.

fo. 97v. *Saint John the Evangelist* (2 3/4 × 2 3/4 in).
the amply draped saint is shown on a background of ruins.

fo. 102r. *Saint John the Evangelist* (2 5/8 × 2 5/8 in).
the saint is shown within a cell. The figure is characterized by a strong monumentality. Behind the saint a window opens onto a landscape.

fo. 118r. *Saint Andrew* (2 5/8 × 2 5/8 in).
the blue cloak and the red book stand out clearly on the dark ground.

fo. 133v. *The Holy Evangelist* (2 5/8 × 2 5/8 in).
the figure of the saint is treated less securely than the others, as though it were the work of a less able hand. The saint is dressed in dark a blue gown with a brown cloak.

fo. 134r. *Saint John the Evangelist* (2 1/2 × 2 5/8 in).
the saint, dressed in a sharp green and a bright red cloak, is represented against a background of ruins.

Bibliography

CATALOG The Renowned Collection of Western mss ... of A. Chester Beatty, 1932, I, p. 58—59, fig. 44;

CATALOG Mostra delle Biblioteche Italiane, 1934, p. 31, no. 100; M. LEVI D'ANCONA, 1950, p. 60, p.

70; G. MUZZIOLI, 1953, p. 399, no. 639; M. LEVI D'ANCONA, 1969, p. 203; M. CIONINI-VISANI, 1971, p. 125, fig. 161, 163, 164, p. 143, no. 35.

VIENNA, Albertina Library, Ms. 2660
Eurialo d'Ascoli's
Stanzas
tempera on parchment

For stylistic reasons the little codex is traditionally attributed to Clovio. The *Stanzas* ware written by Eurialo d'Ascoli, a vernacular poet of the XVI cent. admired by Leo X and friend of Annibal Caro, on the occasion of Charles V's conquest of Tunisia, 1535, and were given to the Emperor in 154; so it is held to have been illuminated within those years. Besides the two complete illuminated sheets (fo. 1v. and fo.2) there are the very beautiful margins (fo. 18 and fo. 19).

fo. 1v. *Allegory of the Catholic Faith* (6 3/8 × 4 in).
The eagle (Charles V) spreads out its talons to protect the nude maiden (the catholic faith) after having fought with two birds in the sky (Tunisia and Algiers. As it relates to the text this interpretation is preferable to the other which has it as the *Death of Dido* (cf. M. G. DE LA COSTE-MESELIERE, 1959). The woman and children in the foreground symbolize *charity*.

fo. 2 *Title of the Work* (6 3/8 × 4 in).
Above the title of the work *Eurialo d'Ascoli's Stanzas on the Venture of Aquila* and the beginning of the stanza there is a rectangular vignette with a *Temple* dedicated to Glory.
Both pages have rich margins of foliage, grotesques, putti, and virile nudes.

Bibliography
R. BEER, 1913, I, p. 42; G. F. WAAGEN, 1850, II, p. 5; J. W. BRADLEY, 1887, I, p. 237; J. W. BRADLEY, 1891 and 1971, p. 312—315; H. J. HERMAN, 1932, p. 176—182; M. G. DE LA COSTE-MESELIERE, 1959, no. 52, p. 5; M. CIONINI-VISANI, 1971, p. 128, fig. 173, 174, p. 142, no. 50.

Head of Minerva,
Windsor Castle, Royal Library

WINDSOR CASTLE, Royal Library, no. 43
Fragments of an illuminated Book of Anthems done in the form of a page
tempera on parchment (26 1/2 × 16 3/4 in)

On the back there are the words of the text and musical notation. Signed *"D. Julio Clovio f."* on a block of stone in the bottom left-hand corner. An anonymous Venetian artist of the XVIII cent. who made a note of a copy of an edition of Vasari's *Vite* printed in Bologna, and in part published by A. Weixlgärter, refers to Vasari's statement that *"At that time he painted a large Chorus Book with fine miniatures"* and adds *"This book has fallen to pieces and has become dispersed because of the negligence of the Abbots of the Order at Candiana, and to my great sorrow I have seen the best figures of the said Book sold for very little and in the homes of dilettanti gentlemen ..."* The fact that an illuminated codex by Clovio (if correctly identified by the annotator as the one remembered by Vasari) was cut up and sold in Northern Italy at the same time in which Consul Smith (fo. 43 comes from his collection) was collecting works by Italian artists could be a coincidence but, it is worth while remembering it. In MS *Catalogue of Paintings, Italian School ...* (in "Burlington Magazine", 1913, p. 161, no. 345) it is described as *"Diverse figures cut out of missals and elegantly posted on cloth and ornamented with gold shading, and in the body of great "P" is drawn Cardinal Grimani visiting Klović in his chamber in the monastery (cm 2,3 × 1,4)"*. If the codex, to which fo. 43 belongs, is the one remembered by Vasari, it must be dated at about 1530, a period which corresponds to the style of the decorations, previous to the declared mannerism of the sure and dated codices (cf. codex Soane and Morgan codex). In fact

Roman mannerism is only seen in the composite stem of the letter "P", the Victory and the cupid that complete the ring, and the little profile of Minerva in the candelabrum in the right-hand margin. All the other elements that form the ornamentation of sheet go back to the humanism of Northern Italy, and the Veneto in particular. For this reason a possible collaboration of Clovio with Gerolamo dei Libri, who was also in the monastery at Canadiana around 1530, is to be considered.

Bibliography
G. VASARI, 1550 and 1568, ed. 1965, VII, p. 441; "Burlington Magazine", 1913, p. 161, no. 345; A. WEXGÄRTER, 1938, p. 128; A. E. POPHAM-J. WILDE, 1949, no. 43; fig. 16; F. VIVIAN, 1971, p. 84 and 195; Catalog, the Queen's Gallery, Buckingham Palace, 1973, p. 59, no. 134; M. CIONINI-VISANI, 1971, p. 123, fig. 162, p. 141, no. 31.

WINDSOR CASTLE, Royal Library, no 243
Head of Minerva
black pencil and grey chalk on paper (11 × 7 7/8 in)

Damaged and carefully repaired along the right margin and Minerva's chin. The attribution is based on the identification of the hand which drew the *Head of Minerva* with that of drawings which are definitely by Clovio, such as the *Adoration of the Kings* (Windsor Castle, no 241) and the signed *Pietà* in London (British Museum, no. 1895-9-15-645). Besides, this drawing corresponds exactly to a small medallion in the margin of fo. 1 of the *Commentary on the Epistle of*

Adoration of the Kings,
Windsor Castle, Royal Library

Saint Paul (London, Soane Museum) done by Clovio between 1537 and 1538. Minerva is wearing a cuirass with the head of Gorgon and a helmet decorated with a scene of a battle between a mounted soldier and a foot soldier.

Bibliography
A. E. POPHAM-J. WILDE, 1949, no. 243; M. CIO-NINI-VISANI, 1971, fig. 170, p. 142, no. 46.

WINDSOR CASTLE, Royal Library, no. 241
Adoration of the Kings
black pencil and grey chalk on paper (12 1/4 × 8 1/2 in)

There is a "G" in pen and black ink at the bottom right which must be considered the beginning of Giulio Clovio's signature. A XVI cent. hand has written "*Giulio Clovio*" in ink on the back. The beautiful drawing fully corresponds to the *Adoration of the Kings* (fo. 38v.) of the *Officium Virginis* at the Morgan Library, New York. The soft pencil-work and the grey shading moderate the well-defined forms and the complicated structures of the scene. For it to be a preparatory study for the miniature (fo. 38v.) at the Morgan Library it must have been done after 1537. An etching by Cornelis Cort, dated 1567, of this drawing exists with only the addition in the second stage of a small *Presentation at the Temple* in the rectangular space near the bottom margin.

Bibliography
J. C. J. BIERENS DE HAAN, 1948, p. 57, fig. 9; A. E. POPHAM-J. WILDE, 1949, no. 241, fig. 52; M. CIONINI-VISANI, 1971, p. 143, no. 63.

*The Virgin, with Child, St. Joseph, St. John the Evangelist and Two
Women*, Windsor Castle, Royal Library

WINDSOR CASTLE, Royal Library, no. 454
Zenobia
black pencil and grey charcoal on paper
(12 1/8 × 9 3/8 in)

The original (Florence, Uffizi, B. B. 1626) is probably
one of the drawings which Michelangelo gave to
Tommaso Cavalieri in 1520. The draftsmanship of the
drawing at Windsor fully reveals the hand of Clovio,
an untiring copyist of Michelangelo. The practically
profile bust of a female figure is adorned in a refined
and complicated way, with her nude breasts supported
by a high sash. To the top right emerges the lightly
sketched head of an old man and at the bottom, also
sketched, that of a child. The title, which is traditionally given to the drawing is certainly inexact. According to Popham it should be identified with the
drawing described in the inventory of Clovio's possessions and published by Bertolotti: *"The fight of
Mars and Venus done by Don Giulio and invented by
Michelangelo".*

Bibliography
M. A. BERTOLOTTI, 1882, p. 12; A. E. POPHAM-J.
WILDE, 1949, no. 454; M. VIONINI-VISANI, 1971,
p. 143, no. 53.

WINDSOR CASTLE, Royal Library, no. 242
*The Virgin with Child, St. Joseph,
St. John the Evangelist and Two Women*
pencil and grey chalk on paper (11 1/8 × 8 1/4 in)

The drawing is very precise and certainly Clovio's. The
figures in the background are probably of his own
invention, while the Virgin and Child derive from the
Madonna which Michelangelo sculpted for the Medici
Chapel from 1521 to 1531. The scene takes place in an
interior suggested only by a window post and a
foreshortening of the cornice of the fireplace.

Bibliography
A. E. POPHAM-J. WILDE, 1949; no . . . 242, fig. 53.

103

Flagellation,
Windsor Castle, Royal Library

WINDSOR CASTLE, Royal Library, no. 451
Flagellation
sanguine on slight traces of black charcoal on paper
the upper corners have been cut (8 × 7 1/4 in)

It bears the inscription *"Julio Clovio da M. Angelo Bon. t"* on the back by the same hand that wrote the inscription on the back of *Tityus* (no. 459 of the same collection) during the XVI cen. *"A Christ at the pillar in red pencil with three of Michelangelo's figures done by Don Giulio"* is listed in the inventory of Clovio's works of 1577 published by Bertolotti. This description corresponds perfectly with the drawing at Windsor, as we need not count the fourth sketched figure to the left which is amply covered by a later figure. Michelangelo's drawing, of which this is the copy, is, as is known, at the base of the *flagellation* by Sebastiano del Piombo in the Church of San Pietro in Montorio, Rome.

Bibliography
M. A. BERTOLOTTI, 1882, p. 14; A. E. POPHAM-J. WILDE, 1949, no. 451.

WINDSOR CASTLE, Royal Library, no. 245
Adoration of the Shepherds
pen, black ink, dark water-color
white lead and sanguine on paper (11 1/4 × 7 7 8 in)

The drawing closely corresponds to the miniature with the *Nativity* (fo. 26v.) of the *Officium Virginis* at the Morgan Library, New York. One can see the gesture of the Madonna, the back of the girl with the basket on her head and the little putti circling in the clouds above. While there are some differences in the borders, this must be considered as a preparatory study for the miniature. The area of light, obtained by taking advantage of the background of the paper, laps the outlines of the strongly chiaroscuro figures creating a dramatic and evocative scene.

Bibliography
A. E. POPHAM-J. WILDE, 1949, no. 245, fig. 54; CATAOLG, *The Queen's Gallery, Buckingham Palace* 1973, p. 58, no. 129; M. CIONINI-VISANI, 1971, p. 143, no. 63.

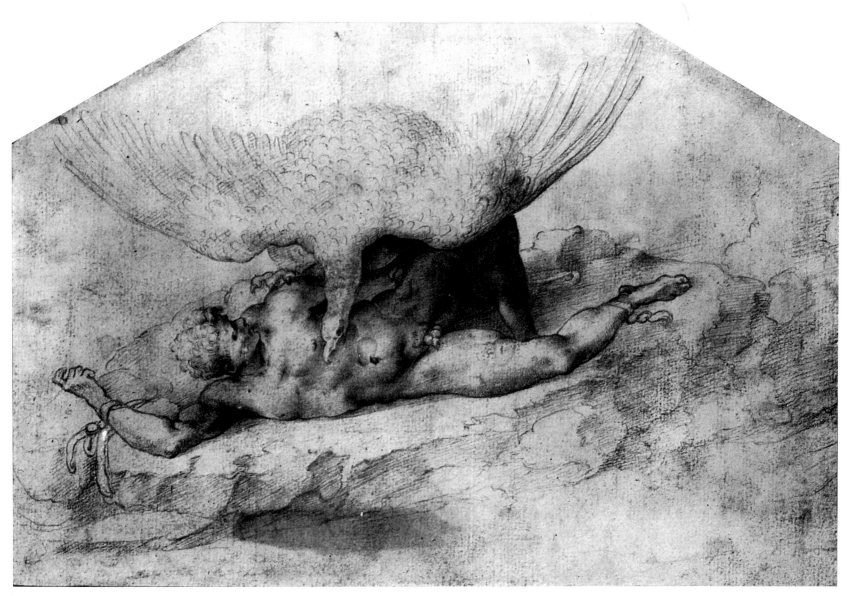

Tityus,
Windsor Castle, Royal Library

WINDSOR CASTLE, Royal Library, no. 459

Tityus
black charcoal and grey chalk on paper
(8 1/8 × 11 1/2 in)

The top corners have been cut. On the back a hand of the XVI cent. has written *"Julio Clovio da M. Angelo Buonarroty"*. The original is drawing no. 429 of the same collection. Clovio's copy closes the group in a statuary isolation; the very curved lines, varying in breadth, have characteristics similar to those of the artist's original drawings and of other copies from Michelangelo (cf. no. 451 and no. 454 at Windsor Castle).

Bibliography

A. E. POPHAM-J. WILDE, 1949, no 459, fig. 104;
M. CIONINI-VISANI, 1971, p. 130, p. 143, no. 53.

WINDSOR CASTLE, Royal Library, no. 457

Ganymede
charcoal and grey chalk on paper (3 5/8 × 10 1/4 in)

Though simpler, the drawing has the usual characteristics, in the line and shading of Clovio's hand. It is generally thought to be the copy of the Ganymede which Michelangelo did, together with the *Tityus,* for the young Tommaso Cavalieri towards the end of 1532. Vasari writes *"The Duke (Cosimo de'Medici) has ... a small picture by the hand of Don Giulio, in which Ganymede is being carried to the heavens by Jupiter turned into an eagle. It was taken from one already drawn by Michelangelo and now in the possession of Tommaso de'Cavalieri ..."*; also Francisco dé Hollanda remembers that *"... Don Giulio showed us a Ganymede iluminated by himself from a drawing by Michelangelo, and treated so softly that it was this the*

Ganymede, Windsor Castle, Royal Library

work which began to give him fame in Rome". Also the 1577 inventory of Clovio's possessions, published by Bertolotti, lists *"The Ganymede by Michelangelo idem id"*.

Bibliography

G. VASARI, 1550/1568, ed. 1965, VII, p. 448; M. A. BERTOLOTTI, 1882, p. 14; A. M. BESSONE AURELI, 1939, p. 159; A. E. POPHAM-J. WILDE, 1949, no. 457, fig. 103; M. CIONINI-VISANI, 1971, p. 130, p. 143, no. 52.

WINDSOR CASTLE, Royal Library, no. 244
The Consignment of the Keys
black ink, dark water-colour charged with white-lead on paper (14 3/8 × 11 1/4 in)

The well-finished drawing has several marks from the damp. It corresponds to a tempera at the Louvre (no. 3044) of the same subject, the only variation being the background. Under the influence of the Michelangelo's frescoes of the Paoline Chapel, the drawing is stylistically very close to the *Conversion of Saint Paul* of the British Museum (no. 1946-7-13-322) and is to be related to the mature period of Clovio's activity.

Bibliography

A. E. POPHAM-J. WILDE, 1949, no. 244.

ZAGREB, Grafički kabinet Jugoslavenske akademije nauka — formerly W. Gernsheim coll. and Gelosi — Lawrence

Judith Putting the Head of Holofernes in her Bag
black charcoal on paper (12 3/4 × 9 1/4 in)

Signed *"Go. Iulio Clovio"* in the bottom left-hand corner. It is very likely the drawing for a miniature — today lost — which is spoken of in a letter, from Rome, written September 11th, 1561, by Annibal Caro to the Duchess Margherita of Parma for Clovio: *"I am sending your highness the painting of Judith finished at last, when God wanted it so. I say this because for as far as my will and solicitude were concerned it would have already been finished months ago ... here it has been seen not without praise for myself and wonder from everyone"*. Clovio called the miniature "painting" because it was a loose composition and not part of a manuscript, and as *"miniatore da gabinetto"* destined to be hung up.
An engraving by Philippe de Soye (cf. Paris, Bibliotheque Nationale) also exists from this sheet.

Bibliography

G. VASARI, 1550 and 1568, ed. 1965, VII, p. 447; I. SAKCINSKI, 1852, p. 48; J. W. BRADLEY, 1891 and 1971, p. 387—388; "Burlington Magazine", 1937, p. 137; J. C. BIERENS DE HAAN, 1848, p. 42; M. CIONINI-VISANI, 1971, p. 143, no. 78.

The Consignment of the Keys,
Windsor Castle, Royal Library

BIBLIOGRAPHY
Works arranged in chronological order

1548   P. PINO *Dialogo della Pittura,* Venice 1548 in P. BAROCCHI, *Trattati d'Arte del Cinquecento,* Bari, 1960/62, I

1550—1568   G. VASARI *Le Vite . . . ,* VII, edited in Milan, 1965 (by G. Previtali, P. Ceschi, F. Negri Arnoli)

1584   R. BORGHINI *Il Riposo . . . in cui della Pittura e della Scultura si Favella,* Florence, 1854

1584   G. P. LOMAZZO *Trattato dell'Arte della Pittura Scultura ed Architettura,* II, edited in Rome, 1584

1619—1621   G. MANCINI *Considerazioni sulla Pittura* (1619/21) in A. MARUCCHI *Fonti e Documenti Inediti per la Storia dell'Arte,* 1, Rome, 1956

1642   G. BAGLIONE *Vite de'Pittori, Scultori, Achitetti dal Pontificato di Gregorio XIII fino a Tutto Quello di Urbano VIII* (dited by V. Mariani, Rome, 1935)

1769   J. J. LALANDE *Voyage d'un Français en Italie, Fait dans les Années 1765/66,* VI, Venice, 1869

1777—1778   J. J. VOLKMANN *Historisch-Kritische Nachrichten von Italien,* III, Leipzig, 1777/78

1818   L. LANZI *Storia Pittorica d'Italia,* Bassano, 1818

1820   F. BORMIAN BERMEJO *Descriptión Aritistica del Real Monastero de San Lorenzo de El Escorial y sus Preciosidades depuisés de la Invasión de los Franceses,* Madrid, 1820

1827   MOREL D'ARLEUX *Inventaire Manuscript des Dessins du Louvre Etabli par Morel, Conservateur du Cabinet des Dessins du Louvre, de 1727 à 1827,* V

1840   F. DE BONI *Biografie Degli Artisti,* Venice 1840

1846/47   F. BALDINUCCI *Notizie de Professori del Disegno da Cimbaue in qua,* V, Ed. IV°, Milan, 1846/47

1850   G. F. WAAGEN *Über ein Manuskript mit Miniaturen des Don Giulio Clovio*, in "Deutsches Kunstblatt" VII, 1850

1852   I. SAKCINSKI (KUKULJEVIĆ) *Leben des G. G. Clovio, Ein Beitrag zur Slavischen Kuntgeschichte* Agram, Suffam, 1852

1852   I. SAKCINSKI (KUKULJEVIĆ) *Lexicon of South Slovenic Artists, Klovio* (ad vocem), 1852

1866   F. REISET *Notice des Dessins, Cartons, Pastels, Miniatures et Emaux Exposés ... au Musee Imperial du Louvre, Première Partie: École d'Italie*, Paris, 1866

1866   A. RONCHINI *Giulio Clovio* in "Atti e Memorie della R. Deputazione di Storia Patria per le Province Modenese e Parmese", IV, Modena, 1965

1870   CATALOGUE of the *Raccolta Santarelli agli Uffizi* Florence, 1870

1882   M. A. BERTOLOTTI *Don Giulio Principe dei Miniatori* in "Atti e Memorie delle Deputazioni di Storia Patria per l'Emilia e per la Romagna", Modena, 1882

1882   M. A. BARTOLOTTI *Don Giulio Clovio, il Principe dei Miniatori*, in "Il Bibliofilo", III, 1882

1884   P. DE NOLHAC *Une Galerie de peinture au XVI siècle: les collections de Fulvio Orsini* in "Gazette des Beaux Arts", 1884

1884   M. MICHIEL (Anonimo Morelliano) in F. MORELLI *Notizie d'Opere del Disegno*, edited by G. Frizzoni, Bologna, 1884

1887   J. W. BRADLEY *Dictionary of Miniaturists*, London 1887

1887   J. L. PROPERT *History of Miniature Art*, London and New York, 1887

1890   P. N. FERRI *I Disegni degli Uffizi*, Florence, 1890

1890   E. MUENTZ *Une Lettre de Don Giulio Clovio à la Duchesse de Parme*, in "Archives des Arts" I, 1890

1891   J. W. BRADLEY *The Life and Works of Giulio Clovio*, London, 1891 (reprinted in Amsterdam in 1971)

1893   I. A. MARESCA *Il Museo del Duca di Marina* in "Napoli Nobilissima" II, April 1893

1905   D. HEATH *Miniatures*, London, 1905

1907   A. RATTI *Guida Sommaria per il Visitatore della Biblioteca Ambrosiana e delle Collezioni Annesse*, Milan, 1907

1912   J. A. HERBERT *Clovio* in "Thieme Becker, Allgemeines Lexikon der Bildenden, "Künstler" VII, 1912, pp. 122—124

1913   R. BEER *La Biblioteca Imperiale di Vienna* in "Bullettin de la Société Française de Réproductions de

1914   V. VON LOGA *Los comiensos de El Greco*, in "La España Moderna" November, 1914

1914   G. JUSTI *Los Comiensos de El Greco*, in "La España Moderna" May, 1914

1914   F. LONGHI *Il Soggiorno Romano di El Greco*, in "L'Arte" 1914

1914   F. DE NAVENNE *Rome, le Palais Farnèse*, Paris, 1914

1917   A. E. BYE *Two Clovio Manuscripts in New York*, in "Art in America", V, February 1917

1920   E. G. MILLAR *Les Manuscrits des Bibliothèques de Londres-Soane Museum*, in "Bullettin de la Société Française de Réproductions de Manuscrits à Peintures" 1914/20

1922   H. KEHRER *Ein Besuch des Giulio Clovio in Atelier Grecos*, in "Kunstchronic und Kunstmarkt" 1922, v. 34°

1922   J. SCHLOSSER *Two Portrait Miniatures from Castle Amras*, in "Burlington Magazine", October 1922

1928   BRITISH MUSEUM *Reproductions from Illuminated Manuscripts*, IV, London, 1928

1929   F. BONNARD *Un hôte du Palais Farnèse. Don Giulio Clovio*, Rome—Paris, 1929

1930   J. ZARCO COEVAS *Inventario de los Albrajos, Relicarios, Estatuas, Pinturas, Tapices y otros Objetos de valor y curiosidad donados por el rey Felipe II al Monasterio El Escorial-Años 1571/98*, in "Boletin de la Real Academia de la Historia" 97°, 1930

1932   H. J. HERMANN *Die Handschriften und Incunabolen der Italianischen Renaissance-3 Mittelitalien: Toskana, Umbrien, Rom*, Leipzig, 1932

1936   A. BICOTICH *G. G. Clovio 1948/1578 (Dalmata?)*, in "Archivio Storico per la Dalmazia" 1936, no. 118

1937   *Old Master Drawings*, a brief note in "Burlington Magazine" March 1937

1938   A. WEIXLGÄRTER *Ein Später Glossator der Vasari*, in "Die Graphischen Künste", III, 1938

1939   A. M. BESSONE AURELI introduction and note to *Francisco De Hollanda, Dialoghi Michelangioleschi (Dialogo IV)*, Rome, 1939

1939   U. MIDDELDORF *Three Italian Drawings in Chicago*, in "Art in America and Elsewhere" 1939, XXVII, no. 1

1939   E. PANOFSKY *Studies in Iconography*, New York, 1939

1940   D. KNIEWAHD *Misal Čazmanskog Prepošta Jurja de Topusko i Zagrebačkog Biskupa Šimuna Erdödy*, Zagreb, 1940

1943   P. PASCHINI *Domenico Grimani, Cardinale di S. Marco (+1523)*, Rome, 1943

1944   D. KNIEWALD *Iluminacija i Datacija Zagrebačkih Liturgijskih Rukopisa*, Zagreb, 1944

1948   J. B. BIERENS DE HAAN *L'Oeuvre gravée de Cornelis Cort, Graveur Hollandais, 1533/1578*, The Hague, 1948

1949   P. D'ANCONA-E. AESCHLIMANN *Dictionnaires des Miniaturistes du Moyen Age et de la Renaissance*, II, Milan, 1949

1949   A. E. POPHAM-J. WILDE *The Italian Drawings of the XV and XVI Centuries in the Collection of His Majesty the King at Windsor Castle*, London, 1949

1949   J. WILDE *The Drawings of Michelangelo and His School*, London, 1949

1950   M. LEVI D'ANCONA *Illuminations by Clovio Lost and Found*, in "Gazette des Beaux Arts" 1950, XXXVII°

1951   G. GALBIATI *Itinerario per il Visitatore della Biblioteca Ambrosiana, della Pinacoteca e dei Monumenti Annessi*, Milan, 1951

1951   J. SUMMERSON *Sir John Soane's Museum*, in "Studio" February 1951

1953   T. H. COLDING *Aspects of Miniature Painting, Its Origins and Development*, Copenhagen 1953

1953   M. HAARSEN-G. K. BOYCE *Italian Manuscripts in the Pierpont Morgan Library*, New York 1953, no. 102

1953 V. MARIANI *Il "Stimmate" di San Francesco del Greco a Napoli* in "Rivista dell'Istituto Nazionale d'Archeologia e Storia dell'Arte", Rome, 1953, vol. II

1954 G. MUZZIOLI *Catalogo della Mostra Storica Nazionale della Miniatura a Palazzo Venezia-Roma*, Florence, 1954

1955 M. SALMI *La Miniatura Italiana*, Milan, 1955

1955 W. SMITH *A Study of the Book of Hours for Cardinal Alessandro Farnese in the Pierpont Morgan Library (M. 69)*, Master's thesis at the Institute of Fine Arts, New York University, May 1955 (unpublished)

1957 F. ZERI *Pittura e Controriforma. L'Arte Senza Tempo di Scipione da Gaeta*, Turin, 1957

1958 E. DUGUE TRAPIER *El Greco in the Farnese Palace*, in "Gazette des Beaux Arts" 1958, I

1959 M. G. LA COSTE-MIESSELIERE *Don Giulio*, in "L'Oeil" 1959, no. 52

1959 J. WILDE *"Cartonetti" by Michelangelo*, in "Burlington Magazine" 1959, CI.

1962 H. E. WHETHEY *El Greco and his School*, Princeton, 1962, II

1963 J. CHENEY *Francesco Salviati's North Italian Journey*, in "Art Bulletin", December 1963

1963 J. WARDROP *The Script of Humanism. Some Aspects of Humanistic Script (1460—1560)*, Oxford, 1963

1964 E. GARELLO-M. BRUCOLI *Il Falso Michelangelo è Risultato un Autentico Clovio* in "Melpomene", 1964, no. 39

1964 W. SMITH *Giulio Clovio and the "Maniera di Figure Piccole"* in "Art Bulletin", September, 1964

1965 CH. DE TOLNAY *Newly Discovered Miniatures by Pieter Brueghel the Elder* in "Burlington Magazine", March 1965

1967 Y. HACKENBROCK *Jewellery of the Court of Albrecht V at Munich* in "Connoisseur", June 1967

1968 J. SCHULZ *Venetian Painted Ceilings of the Renaissance*, University of California, 1968

1969 CATALOGUE *Disegni Italiani e Stranieri del '500 e '600 alla Stanza del Borgo*, Milan, 1969

1969 I. BERKOVITS *Illuminated Manuscripts in Hungary, XI—XVI Centuries*, Budapest, 1969

1969 M. LEVI D'ANCONA *Un Libro Scritto e Miniato da Giulio Clovio* in "Contributi alla Storia del Libro" Biblioteca di Bibliografia Italiana LXII, Florence, 1969

1969 G. MARIANI CANOVA *La Miniatura Veneta del Rinascimento*, Venice, 1969

1970 M. FAGIOLO DELL'ARCO *Il Parmigianino, un Saggio sull'Ermetismo del Cinquecento*, Rome, 1970

1971 F. VIVIAN *Il Console Smith Mercante e Collezionista*, Vicenza, 1971

1973 CATALOGUE *Mostra del'Arredamento del Cinquecento* Vicenza, Palazzo Barbaran Da Porto 1973

1973 CATALOGUE *Drawings by Michelangelo, Raphael and Leonardo and their Contemporaries*. The Queen's Gallery, Buckingham Palace, London, 1973

1973 F. VIATTE-R. BACOU-D. DALLE PIANE PERUGINI CATALOGUE *Mostra del Paesaggio nel Disegno del Cinquecento*, Rome, 1973